How to Elevate Your Life

*Proven Practices to Take Your
Life to the Next Level*

by
Dr. Mark Lantz

How to Elevate Your Life

*Proven Practices to Take Your
Life to the Next Level*

by
Dr. Mark Lantz

LESEA PUBLISHING

South Bend, Indiana

How to Elevate Your Life: Proven Practices to take Your Life to the Next Level
ISBN 1-58568-547-X
Copyright © 2012 by LeSEA Publishing
This Printing September 2012

LeSEA Publishing Co.
A Division of LeSEA, Inc.
530 E. Ireland Rd.
South Bend, IN 46614

www.leseapublishing.com

Contents

Introduction 7

1. The Most Important Decision in
   Life You Will Ever Make 9

2. Character and Credibility 21

3. The Power of Perspective 35

4. Thinking Like a Leader 51

5. Watch Your Language 67

6. What You See Is What You Get 83

7. You Will Never Go Up Until
   You Grow Up 95

8. Coloring Outside the Lines 107

9. Who's Around You Eventually
   Gets in You 121

10. Called to be a Catalyst 141

Conclusion 151

Introduction

Every person has an innate desire to make a difference. No matter the position in which a person finds himself – there is a burning desire within each of us which longs for life to be significant – to matter and count for a greater cause. That is how God created us. None of us want to come to the end of our life with nothing to show of the impact and value we have brought into the world; but rather each of us longs to know that our life mattered, that what we did and who we were in life made a dramatic impression and added value to the people who surrounded us throughout our years on earth. There is a rallying cry that I believe is yearning to emerge from the hearts of so many people. We want our lives to be elevated to the next level. We are discontent to stay where we are and with who we are. Something is pulling at us and urging us to a place where we can become greater and embrace that sense of fulfillment and complete satisfaction. If any of that resonates with you then I invite you to join me on a journey through the pages of this book which will "Elevate Your Life" to the next level. It is a journey in which we carefully and honestly evaluate who we are and where we are in life. It is a journey in which we analyze how our influence is impacting the world around us and what we must do in order to maximize that impact for the greater good of others and most importantly for the glory of God. At the end of your life, what will those closest to you say about you? How will the world have been a better place because of you? In what way will your life have influenced people to become all that they were designed to become? I love this anonymous quote: "When you were born, you cried and the world rejoiced. Live your life so that when you die, the world cries and you rejoice." If that is your desire, then I invite you on this journey with me. Let's respond to that sense of urgency within us to attain to a greater level of significance and worth in our life and leadership. Let's walk and learn together as we choose to "elevate" our lives together!

Chapter One

The Most Important Decision in Life You Will Ever Make

Everyone knows that life is full of decisions. Some decisions are easy to make – others much more difficult with much higher stakes. Some decisions more than others will affect your ability to lead and have influence. Some decisions will be financial, other decisions will be more personal, still others will be directional or visionary decisions. But there is one decision that every effective individual must be willing to make. **The one decision you cannot ignore is the decision to take 100% responsibility for your life.** Unless you are willing to make this decision – no other decision will matter in your life! Unfortunately, we have been accustomed and trained to blame other sources for the parts of our lives that we don't like. When we don't succeed, we like to find some reason or excuse as to why it didn't work out. NCAA football coach

Lou Holtz was so right when he said: "The man who complains about the way the ball bounces is likely the one who dropped it." We blame the economy or lack of the right personnel. We blame our spouse, the weather, our lack of money or resources – anything or anyone we can think of on which to pin the blame. We never really want to admit where the real problem lies…within ourselves.

There is a humorous story told of a man who is out walking one night and comes upon another man down on his knees looking for something under a streetlamp. The passerby inquires as to what the other man is looking for. He answers that he is looking for his lost key. The passerby offers to help and gets down on his knees to help him search for the key. After an hour of fruitless searching, he says, "We've looked everywhere for it and we haven't found it. Are you sure that you lost it here?"

The other man replies, "No, I lost it in my house, but there is more light out here under the streetlamp!"

It is time that you stop looking outside of yourself for the answers to successfull leading. Start realizing that the gift you have to lead has been given to you by God and it is your responsibility to maximize that gift and reach your potential. No one else can do it for you! If it is going to happen it will happen only when you make the decision to stop blaming your past, your background, your lack of training, or any other source for your lack of effectiveness and success. The Apostle Paul was very direct in his exhortation to his young ministry protégée Timothy when he told him, "Wherefore I put thee in remembrance that thou stir up the gift of God, which is in thee by the putting on of my hands." (2 Timothy 1:6) The mentality that Paul possessed was giving a great leadership principle to this young man who had great opportunity lying in front of him: God has given you the gift, but it is your responsibility to use your gift to its fullest potential!

There is a pervasive myth in our world that we are *entitled* to a successful life. Somewhere out in the great beyond, there is someone who is going to bring success, well being, happiness, financial security and all the other things that we want, and drop them into our lap. We look at great people who have accomplished incredible results and we have this myth in our mind that they instantaneously achieved all that they have done and we want the results they have achieved without the effort they have exerted. The fact of the matter is – God has not entrusted anyone else with the results of your life but you! So from the beginning of our time together may we establish this as the primary principle of success – *take 100% responsibility for what you have been given in life and know that the results you achieve will be in direct proportion to the efforts you put forth.*

That is a liberating moment, my friend! Liberating because you have now released every excuse as to why you have not succeeded to this point and realized that you have complete control over using what God has given to you to your full potential. It releases you to be who you are in Christ and stop trying to be someone you are not. You can stop trying to emulate someone else's results and realize that you are unique and special in the sight of God. No one else has the same set of abilities and gifts that you do. Ponder that for just a moment; you are made exactly as God wanted you to be made. He created the set of circumstances in which you were raised. He gave you the set of parents He wanted you to have. He knew when and where He wanted you to be born. There is absolutely nothing in your life that has happened arbitrarily or by accident! God has given you the uniqueness of your personality to fit into His overall purpose for your life. The Psalmist said it well when he wrote: "Thine eyes did see my substance, yet being unperfected; and in thy book all my members were written, which in continuance were fashioned, when as yet there was none of them." (Psalm 119:36) Because these abilities have been uniquely given and designed for us it is completely up to us to use them successfully and become the person you were designed to be. To attempt to be anything else will bring fruitless failure into your life and that is certainly not what you want!

What does taking 100% responsibility for your life really mean? Here are some points for you to consider and put into practice. You will be amazed at the freedom you sense when you actually begin to live out these principles:

You Must Give Up All of Your Excuses

"Ninety-nine percent of failures come from people who have the habit of making excuses." – George Washington Carver

You can no longer play the part of the victim. You cannot talk about all the reasons why you are not where you would like to be in life or leading in the manner of which you know you are capable. It is easy to make excuses but the disciplined person will come face to face with the hard reality as to why he is not where he wants to be and make the needed corrections to alter his course in life and leadership. There is a great quote by John Maxwell which states: "The pessimist complains about the wind. The optimist expects it to change. The leader adjusts the sails." Rather than making excuses, the effective leader will honestly evaluate why he is experiencing the results he is receiving in life and then be willing to adjust whatever needs to change in order to receive different results. If you are unwilling to adjust your way of thinking then you must be content to continue to receive the same results you are receiving. In order to change what you get in life – you must be willing to change who you are in life. The level of your belief affects the level of your behavior. Therefore – to accomplish more you must become more. I have determined that I will work harder on myself than I do anything else.

I will work harder on my <u>person</u> than I do my <u>performance</u>. Rather than try to increase my level of income – I need to increase my level of wisdom. As my wisdom increases so will the opportunity for income. The moment you relinquish all excuses and realize that you are responsible for what happens in your life – you will be free to work at what you <u>can</u> change rather than complain about that which you cannot change. Little in life is more liberating than knowing that there are some things that you just cannot change and it is okay to let them go; because by letting them go you are now free to work on that which you have the power to change. Real progress is made right here!

You Must Be Willing To Change Your Response to People and Situations

The one thing over which you have complete control is your ability to control your response to what happens to you. You cannot control what people say about you. You cannot control the nation's economy. You cannot control what happens to you. But the one thing you can control is how you respond to each of the above situations. Your response to what happens <u>around</u> you will determine the outcome of what happens <u>within</u> you! You cannot control the climate outside but you can control the climate inside your mind. Personal growth is a decision made arbitrarily of the circumstances that surround you.

Many people wait on the perfect opportunity or time in which they will go back to school and get their degree or start working on the project that has lain on the shelf for so long. Now is the time for you to take control over the decisions you are presently making in life. Everything that you experienced in life – both internally as well as externally – is a direct result of how you have responded to what has happened to you in life. Therefore – if you change your decisions you can change the experiences you have in life. Your decisions determine your destiny. What you decide today is what you become tomorrow. You cannot get away from that fact! I have found that there are really only four things over which you have complete control:

- *The thoughts you think*
- *The vision you have for your future*
- *The decisions you make*
- *The actions you take*

Notice the progression of these elements. Your thoughts will determine the level of vision you have for your life. If you continually dwell on negative thoughts then you will have a negative vision for your life, which will then lead to making negative decisions, which will then be translated into negative actions or behavior. Flip the coin over and you will see that when you dwell on positive and proactive thoughts you maintain a clearer vision for your life, which then transcends into right decisions leading to positive actions that will change your life for the good. You have complete control over how you respond to every situation! If you don't like where you are in life then you must change the decision making process that has brought you to this point in life. Your response to life must change if your position in life needs to change. As the well known adage goes: if you keep on doing what you have always done, you will keep getting what you have always gotten! To change what you are <u>receiving</u> in life means you must change what you are <u>doing</u> in life because all outcomes are a direct result of your ability to respond appropriately to what happens in life.

**You Must Refuse To Live With a
Victim Mentality**

You will never live the life you were meant to live as long as you view yourself as a victim. A victim is a person who is held hostage by his or her circumstances or the people who surround them. The more that I talk to people the more I realize that there are too many who feel as if their life is out of their control and there is absolutely nothing they can do about it. They live their lives controlled by external factors; by their boss, their bills, their marriage, their childhood problems and their current situation. As long as you allow external factors to determine who you are in life you will always look at life through the lens of victim. Any time that you feel like your life is spinning out of your control then you have become a victim *because someone or something else is determining the outcome of your life!* That is not how you were designed to live. God has designed you to live with a sense of security and control. How do you know if you are looking at life as a victim? Ask yourself these questions:

- **Do I have a hard time trusting people around me?**

- **Do I make excuses for where I am and who I am in life?**

- **Do I find myself blaming other people or circumstances for the lack of achievement in my life?**

- **Has my spiritual growth been stagnated because of my lack of faith in what God can do in my life?**

If any of these resonate with you then it is time to make a change. From this moment on take complete responsibility for everything you are today. Take responsibility for everything you think, say, do, and become from this moment forward. If you are to succeed then you must begin fully walking in your position of complete spiritual authority. In other words – you will not allow outward circumstances to determine whether or not you do what God has called you to do. Whether you succeed or fail completely depends on your willingness to allow God to work out His plan in your life as well as your willingness to accept complete responsibility to follow that plan. That is why Paul the Apostle exhorts us in Philippians 2:12-13 "...work out <u>your own salvation</u> with fear and trembling; for it is God who works in you both to will and to do for His good pleasure."

It was this same apostle who along with Silas made the choice that a cold night in a Philippian prison would not determine whether or not they fulfilled the plan of God to preach the Gospel for "... at midnight Paul and Silas were praying and singing hymns to God." (Acts 16:25)

Many of you are facing challenging circumstances in your life right now. You are presently surrounded by challenging people who have become a hindrance to the reaching of your potential. Realize today that you cannot control those circumstances and neither can you control those people – stop trying to because it will never happen. But do not lose the one thing you can control which is your ability to navigate through those challenging circumstances with the grace and wisdom of God. Take responsibility. Step up and shout to the world "I can do this by the grace of God." Tell yourself in the mirror every morning "I will make it past this challenge." Because the bottom line is this: **Your destiny is not decided by the challenging events**

or people with which you are surrounded. Your destiny is determined by your ability to embrace the challenge and use it to your advantage. If you are to succeed at becoming the person who God intended for you to be then it is time that you take honest inventory of where you are in life. Results don't lie – they are only a mirror of the choices and decisions you have made up to this point in your life. If you don't like what you are seeing in the mirror then it is time for you to see why your life looks the way that it does. James illustrates this principle so well when he wrote: "But be doers of the word, and not hearers only, deceiving yourselves. For if anyone is a hearer of the word and not a doer, he is like a man observing his natural face in a mirror; for he observes himself, goes away, and immediately forgets what kind of man he was." (James 1:22-24)

It is what you do that creates the results you see in the mirror. When you look in the mirror of your life, what do you see? Are you satisfied with your present level in life? Are you where you thought you would be at this age and season of your life? Are you accomplishing all that you thought you would be accomplishing by this time? Is your spiritual level of living where you would like it to be? Are you physically in the position you think you should be? Is your life earmarked by satisfaction and fulfillment? What do you really see when you look in the mirror?

Only action can change what you see. Hoping for it and dreaming about it will change nothing. Having

19

the greatest vision for your life will accomplish little unless you resolve to step up and do that hard work of changing what you <u>do</u> in order to change who you <u>are</u>. Do whatever is necessary for your life to make a turn for the better. Start paying attention to what is happening around you and how people are responding to you. This is a great moment for you – don't miss the chance to make dramatic changes. Elevating your life begins with making the most important decision you will ever make: take complete responsibility for your life!

Chapter Two

Character and Credibility

You are about to read a statement that may on the surface seem incredulous; but here is a reality check: *Character is not essential to leadership.* There are leaders of whom we all know who have led large ministries and organizations garnering the loyalty of many followers yet lacked character. Adolf Hitler was a leader with an entire nation following him but was he really worth following? Jim Jones was an infamous leader who led 918 people to their death on November 18, 1978 in the northwestern Guyana community known as "Jonestown". He had a following – but was he a leader worth following? These examples along with many others of leadership without character abound everywhere. You see it in politics – you see it in business – you see it in ministry. The bottom line is: You may be able to lead without character, but character is what makes you a leader <u>worth</u> <u>following</u>. You may lack skills and abilities in many areas – but the one attribute that must be in your portfolio of leadership and personal success is character. Without character, you will always find yourself on the wrong side of your potential.

In an address to the Corps of Cadets at the U.S. Military Academy, General H. Norman Schwarzkopf spoke about the importance of leadership and service. Schwarzkopf said, "I've met a lot of leaders in the Army who were competent, but they didn't have character. And for every job they did well, they sought reward in the form of promotions, in the form of awards and decorations, in the form of getting ahead at the expense of someone else, in the form of another piece of paper that awarded them another degree, a sure road to the top."

You may achieve great accomplishments causing people to recognize your name, but it is your character which determines what people <u>associate</u> with your name. Your abilities may determine your potential, but it is your character that decides your legacy. Your skills may create a luxurious and enviable lifestyle, but you cannot create a life worth living without giving serious thought to the issue of character and who you really are. It is not about making a <u>living</u> – it is about creating a <u>life</u>! The more you change then the more everything around you will change. Far too many of us are depending on <u>circumstances</u> to determine our level of success when we should be depending on our character. Character remains the same regardless of the circumstance. You cannot put your *"finger to the wind"* to see which direction you plan to navigate the ship of your life – you should already know the course that you have chosen to follow and even if the wind blows against you – you still sail in the direction of character and integrity, for those are values that do not change with the direction of the social winds of the world around you. In order to lead people you must first be able to lead yourself. The man who cannot lead himself is not fit to lead others. Therefore – take these thoughts to heart:

Character Is a Choice

The person you are today is the sum total of all the choices and decisions you have made in life up to this point. As we have already discussed in the first chapter – you are responsible for who you are and you cannot lay blame on anyone or anything else in your life. 19th Century clergyman Henry Ward Beecher said: "Hold yourself responsible for a higher standard than anyone else expects of you. Be a hard master to yourself and be lenient to everyone else." Each time that you make the hard decision to do what is right you strengthen your character and integrity. You become a person with laser sharp focus that is able to navigate through difficult situations because you have a set of values that is unbending and unwavering. People begin to respect you because they know what to expect out of you. The converse is true as well: each time you make a decision to take the easy way – the way of compromise that goes against your values and beliefs – you weaken your character. You start sliding down a slippery slope that many times becomes almost impossible to climb back up. What you decide daily determines who you become permanently. Someone once said that men rarely choose their future – they simply choose their habits and their habits decide their future. Look at the decisions you have made today. Are they consistent with the values in which you believe? If you value your physical health – why have you not made the decision to exercise on a regular basis and stop eating unhealthy junk food before going to bed? If you value the people with whom you live – why do you sit in front of the television from the moment you get home from work until the evening is over? If you value your ability to influence people in a positive manner – why haven't you enrolled in a seminar that will teach and inspire you to become better at what you do? You see character has very little to do with what you say; it has everything to do with who you are. If what you say and who you are don't match then you have missed this ever important ingredient of character.

Character Means You Are
Complete – Not Perfect

The dictionary defines integrity as "the quality or state of being complete or undivided". It means that you are not at war with yourself. What you say matches what you do. You are who you are, no matter where you are or who you are with. Integrity allows you to predetermine what you will be regardless of the circumstance, people involved, or the place of your testing. You are not a "human doing" – you are a "human being". Those who live a dualistic lifestyle not only lack integrity but they are also very miserable people! Every person lives and leads on two fronts: a visible front and an invisible front. The visible front relies on your position and title. It is what people think you are and what you say you are. But the invisible front relies on your moral authority. Your position or title will only allow you to lead so far or within a certain spectrum such as your office or your pulpit. Whereas your moral authority awards you authority in a variety of contexts – basically anywhere you may go and live. Moral authority is not something you are given – it is something you have earned. It is the credibility you earn by walking your talk. It is the unity that other people see between what you allege you are to what you really are. When your level of behavior is completely synchronized with your level of belief then you are a person of integrity;

you live in complete unity and not disharmony with yourself. You will never be perfect until you reach your eternal destiny in heaven. Start focusing more on being certain that your lifestyle matches and agrees with your values; for integrity leads you to completeness.

Image and Integrity Are Not the Same Thing

Many people are more worried about their <u>image</u> then they are their <u>integrity</u>. They make decisions based on what they imagine other people are going to think and feel rather than based on what is right. It is like standing in front of the mirror looking at your image. What you see in the mirror looks like you – yet you are not really in the mirror – it is only a reflection of the real you. Therefore your image in leadership is not really you either – it is only what people see about you and think about you. So the hard question you must be able to answer is this: Do you spend more time trying to fix up what people are seeing or thinking about you than you do trying to fix up who you really are? Many leaders will pay huge amounts of money to hire image consultants that will transform everything from their physical appearance to their ability to stand in front of large audiences and deliver a speech.

Rather than consult with an "underline expert" on how to improve his image – a good leader will consult with himself on how to improve his integrity.

They look deep inside of their spirit to make certain that what they portray on the outside is an accurate picture of who they are on the inside. They do not distort the truth in any way but other people know that what they see is accurate and true. Image is a mirage but integrity is the real thing. Your image will not get you through difficult times because it quickly fades when your life is put to the test. But integrity shines brightly when life brings you a test because it is through those same tests of life that integrity and character is not only developed, but most brilliantly demonstrated. The Apostle James said it well when he wrote James 1:2-3, "My brethren, count it all joy when ye fall into divers temptations; Knowing this, that the trying of your faith worketh patience. But let patience have her perfect work, that ye may be perfect and entire, wanting nothing." To be entire means to be complete; there is nothing missing. Isn't it ironic that through the difficult times of life your completeness is accomplished? Integrity shines brightest in the darkest days of your life; which leads me to this next point…

Character Will Be Tested

It is only when the pressure is applied and you are

forced to make a decision to either live consistently with your values or compromise your values that you will have the ability to reveal your real character. Character is not an issue of discussion – it is an issue of demonstration. What we talk about means nothing until our words have been put to the test of whether our <u>works</u> will match our <u>words</u>. That is obviously what the Lord had in mind when He prompted James through the Holy Spirit to write: "What doth it profit, my brethren, though a man say he hath faith, and have not works? Can faith save him? Yea, a man may say, Thou hast faith, and I have works: shew me thy faith without thy works, and I will shew thee my faith by my works." (James 2:14, 18) Every test of your character is an opportunity to do well and live according to your set of determined values. But realize this: the moment you decide to live with integrity is the moment you must accept the fact that you will be tested. Because character that is not tested is character that is not true!

What made the Old Testament character Joseph such a great man is that in the moment he could have sacrificed his integrity for a moment of pleasure with the beautiful wife of his employer – he chose to sacrifice his image so that he could maintain his integrity. It has been said many times: Joseph may have lost his coat – but he never lost his character. When you choose integrity over image you are developing a resolve within your heart that will one day lead you to stand before great men. When you decide that honesty will be a value by which you are defined then expect to have that honesty challenged on the job by being asked to misrepresent figures or expectations for the "sake of the company." When you decide that physical health is important enough to you to change your diet then you can expect invitations to enjoy greasy cheeseburgers and fries to be on the rise! When you decide that your spiritual walk with God will become stronger through prayer and meditation in the Word, know that your willingness to rise 30 minutes earlier to pray and study will be tested by the warmth and coziness of your blankets. When the decision to live with character and integrity is put to the test and you prove yourself true to your decision; it is then that your <u>resolution</u> becomes a <u>revolution</u> that totally changes your life. All of life is a test. Character cannot be taught through a seminar or class; it must be developed through difficulty and challenges.

Character Will Produce

There is definitely a cost to character. There is a high price that must be paid for those who desire to walk in integrity. There are individuals who have lost their jobs because they refused to agree and advocate the dishonest and unethical practices of those in authority in their business. I personally had a friend whose wife left him after he became a Christian because of the dramatic change that took place in his behavior and lifestyle; so dramatic was the change that she walked out on their marriage. But despite the <u>cost</u> of character the <u>reward</u> of character is much greater.

Character produces a greater sense of self worth. When you make the right choices and you do the hard thing rather than the easy thing, you then feel better about yourself. You view yourself with greater respect and when you respect yourself, you invite respect from others as well. Living with integrity rewards you the ability to look at yourself in the mirror at night before you retire for the day and be proud of what you see. You can squarely look yourself in the eye and know that you have done the right thing. You have made the right choice to pursue a life of hard work and diligence rather than one full of ease and laziness. An individual who cannot maintain a healthy esteem of himself will never be highly esteemed by others. Your *net* worth is determined by your *self* worth. Build how much you are worth by living with integrity and character.

Character produces respect from the world around you. In spite of the fact that we live in a world where ethics have seemed to become a byword to be cast alongside the road; the reality is that most people have great respect for those who refuse to compromise their values. There is an innate desire within humans to stand strong and be resilient. Unfortunately, the majority of our world has taken the path of least resistance; so when they see someone willing to sacrifice his image in order to maintain his integrity there is something within them that rises up and cheers because that is really how they want to be. You know how it is when you are watching a movie and the Super Hero comes and vanquishes the villain causing good to triumph over evil – we all get excited and want to be like that Super Hero. Choosing character over convenience creates a deep respect in the hearts and minds of those who are watching your life.

Character produces consistency. When you decide ahead of time how you will behave in every circumstance and situation by determining your values then people will know what to expect from you no matter what you are facing. No one likes the unexpected. You don't enjoy walking into your place of employment only to see and hear the ranting and raving of a boss who has lost control of his emotions. No child wants to be hugged by a parent who just yesterday screamed at them for being incompetent and incapable. People like to know what they can expect out of you from day to day. They like to know that your behavior is consistent because *consistency breeds confidence.* When you treat people with respect one day and then the next day treat them as if they are worthless garbage, you destroy their level of confidence. When you are friendly one day only to show up the next day with a scowl on your face – people will not know how or even when to approach you and will lack the needed confidence to interact with you. I have a select number of restaurants at which I enjoy eating and there is a reason for that. Each time that I go I know that I will be treated with not only great service, but also great tasting food. One of the restaurants that was on that list recently gave us a bad experience as the food had seemingly lost its level of quality and taste to my wife and me. Thinking that it may simply have been a down day for the staff I tried the restaurant again only to find the same disappointment in the quality of food. By now, serious doubts about this restaurant remaining on my top ten list had begun to plague my mind due to having back to back negative experiences. I gave the establishment one more shot a few months later only again to realize that this no longer attracted our palate like it once did; quite honestly we have not been back since that time. What happened? They lost their consistency. It doesn't take long for people to receive a "bad taste" in their mouth when they don't see consistent character and integrity from your life. They need to know what to expect from you day in and day out. The only way for people to know what to expect is for you to live according to what you know. Live by your values and you will never lack consistency because your set of values is the only thing that does not change in the midst of an ever changing society.

Character is the Greatest Victory
You Will Ever Win

Every leader likes to win. I don't know of any leader who enjoys failing or falling short. It is the DNA of each great man or woman in leadership to triumphantly rise above challenges and inspire those who are following them to do the same. There is fulfillment that comes from knowing that you have been able to inspire others to reach their potential. But leading others to their potential is not the greatest act of leadership a person will ever experience. Motivating others to become great is not the highest goal of every leader. Living a life of character and integrity will lead you to the greatest victory you will ever win as a person – that is the victory over yourself. The Apostle Paul fought this battle with determination and resolve as evidenced by what he wrote to us in 1 Corinthians 9:26-27: "I therefore so run, not as uncertainly; so fight I, not as one that beateth the air: But I keep under my body, and bring it into subjection: lest that by any means, when I have preached to others, I myself should be a castaway." The Apostle knew that the enemy within him was very real and that no one else could fight this battle for him – he had to fight it himself because **he** was the enemy! Ralph Stayer, president of Johnsonville Foods, wrote: "In most situations, I am the problem. My mentalities, my pictures, my expectations form the biggest obstacles to my success." I believe that

Mr. Stayer had it right and was feeling what many of us feel throughout our lifetime. We find that the biggest enemy is not our boss – not our spouse – and not our greatest critic; it is ourselves. But living with character and integrity gives you the power to overcome the greatest adversary you will ever face: that inner person who will fight against what you know is right because doing the right thing requires discipline and by nature humans are not disciplined creatures. Predetermining your set of values and making the decision that no matter what happens you plan to live by these values and be the same person regardless of where you are or who you are with will award you great victory. In fact it minimizes the struggle and fight in that moment of choice because you have already made the decision of who you are and how you will live. When you make the choice while the pressure is off your resolve to do right will rise when the pressure is on. Character equals credibility. Character matters. Character is what makes the difference. Resolve today to be the man or woman of character who stands out from the rest; then expect your life to be elevated to an entirely different level!

Chapter Three

The Power
of Perspective

Perspective is everything. Before God ever
moves you into a new season of your life He first
must change your perspective because how you
perceive things will determine how you respond to
things; and how you respond to things determines
the results you get out of life. I am personally at a
point in my life where I am closely evaluating where
I am in life and what I have been able to accomplish
with the years that God has given to me. Through
that personal analysis and evaluation I have realized
that the reason I have not accomplished more than
I have is because I have had an improper perspective on the most significant issues that deal with my
leadership. I have personally realized that until I
change the way that I view leadership – I will never
change my approach to leadership. Of all the issues
discussed in this book – perspective rises to the top

on my personal list of changes that must be made if I plan to elevate my life to the next level. When a man changes his perspective he releases a power within himself that will change not only who he is but most importantly what he accomplishes. Spend a few moments with me discovering the power of your perspective and how just a few alterations to the way you view leadership can bring drastic change into your life and the lives of the people with whom you interact.

Examine The Perspective of Your Purpose

I played football in high school and was privileged to play under a great high school coach who was very successful. Each day as we would come to practice the coach and one of his assistants would climb high above the field on special scaffolding from which he would watch the team scrimmage for that particular practice. This is obviously a common and accepted practice among coaches at all levels and the reason these coaches do this each practice is very easy to understand: climbing above the practice field allows you to see things from a different perspective. The coach is able to see offensive linemen who may be missing their blocking assignments; or he may see a running back who needs to be hitting the hole a little quicker than he does; or he may see that if a receiver would just get a quicker start off the line he would be able to gain a step on the defensive back. Sometimes it takes the coach getting "off the field" and away from the action to be able to see things that he would not be able to see at ground level. Literally raising his perspective allows the coach to make needed changes to his team because he sees the performance of the team from a different perspective whereby the entire team becomes better; all because of a change in the coach's perspective. There are times in your life when you need to step away from the action on the field of your life in order to gain a new perspective of what is happening. I know how busy you can get in living and leading and it seems as though the days begin to roll together without any thought on whether you are living and leading in the sphere and with the style God wants you to lead. You get so taken up in the "play by play" action of creating and communicating vision; articulating the logistics of how things need to be done; managing personnel and trying to develop other leaders that you forget to review and if needed renew your perspective of why you do what you do. Your purpose in life must be your priority. There is nothing more important for you to both discover, as well as develop, the purpose for which you have been created and placed upon this earth. Mark Twain said: "The two most important days of your life are the day you are born and the day you find out why." Without purpose everything becomes meaningless and mundane. You must constantly reevaluate why you do what you do because there is power in the defining and the development of your purpose. Every successful person can clearly articulate the purpose behind what they do and who they are in life. It is that purpose that not only defines you, but also drives you through the sometimes mundane and laborious tasks of getting to where you need to be in life. The person who understands the why or the purpose of what they do will always far exceed the person who merely goes through the motions of everyday living. A man or woman driven by purpose is willing and able to endure almost any negative or adversarial circumstance if he or she clearly understands the <u>why</u> behind what they do. A beautiful illustration of this is a story I once heard of two warring tribes that both lived in the Andes Mountains – one lived in the lowlands and the other tribe lived high in the mountains. One day the mountain tribe invaded the tribe in the lowlands plundering the village and cruelly kidnapping a baby from that village. They disappeared from the village taking the innocent baby with them high up into the mountains to their village home. The tribal people from the lowlands were shocked and outraged at the kidnapping of one of their own; yet stymied by the fact that they did not know how to climb the mountains or track the tribe who had aggressively brought this tragedy to them. The lowlanders did not know the trails that led to the mountain tribe and they were very unfamiliar with the terrain. Yet, because this baby was one of their own – the best fighting men of the lowland tribe got together and formed a search party to go and bring this baby home. The men first tried one method of climbing and then another. They tried one trail but when that trail led nowhere they tried another set of trails. After several days of fruitless effort, however, these men had climbed only a few hundred feet. Feeling discouraged and despondent, the lowlander tribe decided that this was a lost cause and they made preparation to return to their village below. Just as they were packing their gear and preparing for their descent back down into their village, they suddenly saw the baby's mother walking toward them down from the mountain that these strong and able fighting men had been unable to climb. They saw that this mother had the baby strapped to her back and these men were amazed at the strength and resolve of this woman. The men asked her how she was capable of climbing the mountain that the strongest and most able men of the tribe were unable to climb. She looked sternly and intently at them and replied: "It wasn't your baby." When you know why you do what you do then you will be able to climb the highest mountain; swim the deepest ocean; scale the most difficult terrain to accomplish your purpose. It is essential that you approach everything you do from the perspective of purpose. Be willing to ask yourself the hard question of the exact reason why you do everything that you do. One practice I have tried to develop with the team of leaders with whom

I am privileged to work is that before we ever plan an event or a project we must first develop a clear and compelling reason why we are planning and conducting this event or project. There is a form that each leader must complete and evaluate asking such urgent questions as: Why is this being done? What would you like to see as a result of this event? What would "on purpose" really mean to you for this event? What are your primary goals and objectives for this event? How will you know that it is successful? After these questions have been answered we then brainstorm by evaluating the following: What are all the things that occur to me about this event? What haven't I considered and what should I consider? It is only after these questions are answered that we create lists of all that needs to be done in order to reach our goals and fulfill our purpose. We can then move into the phase of looking at all things we can immediately do to start the process of making this event successful. Now, if this works for a team of leaders organizing and planning an event or project then why can't this work for you in organizing and planning your personal life? Your <u>life</u> and <u>ability</u> to lead is the biggest event and project you will ever create; therefore investing the time to gain a clear perspective about who you are and the purpose behind what you do is imperative if you plan to be successful in your life and leadership. Your life is not worth living if you do not invest the time to evaluate the driving force behind all that you do.

You may be surprised to find out what drives you. Be certain that you cultivate a proper perspective of your purpose in life. You may have heard the terms of "efficiency" and "effectiveness" used as a part of management and leadership language. But even in your personal life it is extremely important to know the difference between the two. Efficiency refers to doing things right. Effectiveness, on the other hand, refers to doing the right things. It constantly measures if the actual output meets the desired output. If you take the proper perspective of your purpose it will give you the power to discern between what you should be doing and those things that do not fit into your overall purpose. Perspective gives you the power to say "yes" to the right things and courage to say "no" to the wrong things. The worst thing you can do is find yourself caught in the maze of activities that are not adding value to your overall purpose and value in life. The wise and effective person will have the discernment needed to see the difference between the good and the best. Not all good activities are the right activities. Stop and evaluate the following right now: *What are you doing that is not moving you closer to your overall purpose? What are you doing that is outside of your strength zone of gifts and abilities? What are you doing that someone else could do which would enable you to do the things that only you can do? How does what you are doing contribute to the overall picture of what you desire to achieve and accomplish within your lifetime?* Start now to look at every activity in your life through the lens of purpose and be certain to move forward only on the things that contribute to your overall purpose and wellbeing. You will be amazed at the decrease in the level of stress when you start viewing life through this perspective. Not only will it change who you are but it will also dramatically change what you do. Your perspective of purpose is extremely vital to your success.

Examine Your Perspective of People

The Bible encourages us with these words in Ecclesiastes 4:9: "Two are better than one; because they have a good reward for their labour." There is reward in relationships and the cultivation and collection of right relationships is the key that unlocks the door of success and prosperity. Later in this book we will take some time to discuss the power in your partners and inner circle but right now I feel it is extremely important to take a moment to consider the perspective you have toward people because your perspective makes the decision of how you will treat them; and how you treat them determines what value they will add to your life. Relationships are about productivity; but you can only produce with someone of whom you have the right perspective. Consider the following as you evaluate where your perspective of people lay:

Be convinced that all people have potential. I operate my life with the firm belief that if people will only believe in what God has placed within them that they have the opportunity to reach their complete potential and become everything that God created them to be. Since all people were created in the image of God with a divine purpose and plan for their lives they have the same opportunity that you have to reach that potential and fulfill that purpose. Even the man in the worst of circumstances can radically change his life in an instant by a simple decision to move from the damaging decisions he has made that have led him to his present position to better decisions that lead to a better tomorrow. Any man can change his thinking from where he is today to a better mindset for his tomorrow. Most people have not found that purpose nor have they fully understood their potential simply because no one has taken the time to invest in them and inspire them to reach beyond who they are in order to become who they are destined to be. That is why when I interact with people I treat them as one who has a "10" over his head. I don't base this on what they look like or their present position in life. I base this on the fact that I know every person has been created by the same God Who created me; and if God has placed within me the propensity to change and become someone great then God has done the same for them. Therefore, you should treat them as someone who has the capacity to become someone greater than they are at the present moment. If you treat people as they are then they will never change because there is no motivation to change. But if you treat people as if they already are what they can potentially become; they then have the motivation to live up to the level at which you are treating them. People are more inclined to change because of a motivator rather than a dictator. If you can motivate people to change through creating a clear picture of the reward that will come as a result of that change then you will never struggle with people wanting to make positive changes in their lives. The best way to motivate them is to treat them as if they already live at the level of which you believe they are capable of living. I like to follow Paul's ideology that he used with the Philippians as he wrote in his letter to them: "...being confident of this very thing, that He who has begun a good work in you will complete it until the day of Jesus Christ." (Philippians 1:6) Have a perspective that all people have potential.

Everybody wants to be somebody. There is an innate hunger in every person for applause and recognition. People simply want to know that their life matters and carries at least a small significance. People want to know that who they are and what they do is in some way contributing to the greater good of a world that is much bigger than themselves. Whether people realize it or not, every day they find themselves immersed in an endless struggle to find significance and meaning. That is why you see people doing crazy things just to get the attention of people around them; it all stems from a cry for us to recognize that they are somebody. It was said that Oliver Wendell Holmes was walking down a street one day and a little girl joined him. When the girl started to turn back home, the famed jurist said, "When your mother asks you where you've been, tell her you've been walking with Oliver Wendell Holmes."

"Okay," said the girl confidently, "and when your folks ask you where you've been, tell them you were walking with Mary Susanna Brown." I love the level of self esteem in that little girl! Everyone wants to be somebody; so you must strive to cultivate that desire that is already within the heart of people. Put people in a position where you know they can succeed. Encourage them in their area of natural gifting and ability. Encourage them when they do something right; gently and constructively correct them when they do something wrong. When you begin to see people through the lens of the fact that they want to be somebody then you will begin to see that you are the person that can unlock that desire and really make them that "somebody"!

People are interested in the person who shows genuine interest in them. You must consistently ask yourself if you are more focused on your interests than you are the interest of other people. Let's be very honest with each other; the greatest question every person has is "What's in it for me?" People are not interested in what you are interested in; they are only concerned about what sparks a fire inside of them. Therefore, if you can somehow unlock that door that hides their interests and get people talking about themselves and what is of significance to them, then you will have a friend for life. The most boring people are those who are intoxicated with their own sense of importance and do nothing but talk about themselves and their accomplishments. Since people talk about what they think about it must be concluded that people who only talk about themselves must consequently only think about themselves! In order to conduct a healthy conversation, which in turn may lead to a lifelong healthy relationship, you must focus on the other person more than yourself. Be willing to ask questions and then listen carefully to their responses. Be fully engaged in what is important to them. People do not want to hear what you have accomplished; they merely want you to be interested in what they have accomplished. Show that level of interest and you will have gained the respect of every person you attempt to lead in life. When people respect you they will respond to what you tell them to do. If you want people to disrespect you and consequently not follow you then talk about yourself all the time; interrupt people when they are talking because you feel like your idea and thought is more important than what they have to say; and never listen too long to what others are saying because surely you are much more important than they are.

I guarantee you will be mocked and laughed at and most tragically never receive the respect that every leader needs to be successful. Have the perspective that people will be interested in you if you are interested in them.

Enthusiasm is contagious – be a carrier. That statement is on my personal statement of values and I make certain that when I deal with people I do so with enthusiasm because I have found people respond better to enthusiasm than they do criticism or anything else. People respond more to a smile than they do a frown. A smile is inviting. It opens the door of your life to people and lets them know that it is okay to respond to you. Think about it: when you see someone frowning and unenthusiastic your natural inclination is to avoid that person and stay away. But when someone is smiling with enthusiasm exuding from them it is as if they are telling you to come into their life because there is a gift they have to give to you. That gift is enthusiasm! I am naturally optimistic and I know that I have at times gone a little "overboard" with my optimism. But I have also realized that in an age of such pessimistic and negative news of world events people are longing for just a taste of good news and optimism. You are that outlet and channel that people are looking for! Change your perspective and start seeing people through the lens of enthusiasm. They will feel better and so will you!

Examine the Perspective of Your Person

How you see yourself dramatically influences how you see others. Those with an unhealthy and low self esteem will have an unhealthy and low view of other people. People who have a very healthy and high esteem of themselves will see others through that same set of lenses. I like the story that John Maxell tells in his book **Winning With People**. A traveler nearing a great city asked an old man seated by the road, "What are the people like in this city?"

"What were they like where you came from?" the man asked.

"Horrible," the traveler reported. "Mean, untrustworthy, detestable in all respects."

"Ah," said the old man, "you will find them the same in the city ahead." Scarcely had the first traveler gone on his way when another stopped to inquire about the people in the city before him. Again the old man asked about the people in the place the traveler has just left.

"They were fine people: honest, industrious, and generous to a fault," declared the second traveler. "I was sorry to leave."

The old man responded, "That's exactly how you'll find the people here." The way people see others is a reflection of who they are. If you are a trusting person you will see others as trustworthy. If you are a critical person then you will see others as critical. If you are a caring person then you will see others as compassionate. Your personality comes through when you talk about others and interact with them. Someone who doesn't know you would be able to tell a lot about who you are based on simple observation. It is extremely important to make yourself healthy before you try to make anyone else healthy. You cannot effectively help others feel valuable without first having a positive perception of your own self worth. Most of the problems you will encounter in leadership will be caused by people who are engaged in this endless struggle to think well of themselves. They have never worked through the difficult circumstances of past experiences or relationships; therefore they take an attitude of criticism and denigration with them wherever they go in life. You will limit your ability to lead if you are one of those people. Take the time to examine how you feel about yourself.

Perspective is everything. If you will take the time to examine and be willing to change your perspective then your entire approach to life and leadership will dramatically increase for the good. You get one shot at this so why not give it your best! I challenge you to evaluate the lens through which you view your purpose – other people – and yourself and realize that how you see things determines how you take action. Take action with the right perspective today!

Chapter Four

Thinking
Like a Leader

Great thinkers are great leaders. Note that I didn't say deep thinkers or even philosophical thinkers. Great leaders are those who intentionally choose to fill their mind with great things not small things. Small thoughts are the enemy of big dreams. Neither can big thoughts grow in small minds. Therefore, in order for you to elevate your life, you must choose to use your mind to envision a greater life; an uncommon life; one that is vastly beyond what you have ever experienced. Consider this passage of Scripture with me for a moment. The Lord told the Israelites in Deuteronomy 28:13 "And the LORD will make you the head and not the tail; you shall be above only, and not be beneath…" What does the head do? It thinks – it makes decisions. When you walk in obedience to God He will bring the blessing of great thinking into your life enabling you to lead others due to the decisiveness and direction of your life.

Every person wants to follow someone who knows where they are going.

People who are decisive about their direction are those who have taken the time and developed the art of great thinking.

Leaders Think Differently Than Followers

As long as you have the mindset of a follower you will always be on the tail end looking to someone else for direction. You will always be asking "What comes next?" rather than declaring "This is what happens now!" Change your mindset and decide to be a great thinker and you will be out in front leading and enjoying the view that no one else will see until later! That is what makes people leaders. They see things before everyone else because they are out in front with their thinking which in turn puts them out in front with their leadership as well. Followers always wait for instructions of what comes next while leaders are the ones who have already evaluated the situation and decided what comes next. The most valuable thing a person needs to know is what to do next in every situation. If you have the ability to see the next logical step in any given solution then you will never lack for followers. The thing that will set you apart as a leader is that you have the ability to distinguish the difference between what <u>can</u> be done and what <u>must</u> be done. Leaders are the ones who make things happen while followers stand around and wonder what just happened! You will think like those you hang with which is why you find leaders spending time with other leaders. One of my all time favorite stories is the story of the eagle and the prairie chicken. There was a large majestic mountainside on which a fragile eagle's nest rested. The eagle's nest contained four large eagle eggs. One day an earthquake rocked the mountain causing one of the eggs to tumble down the mountain to a chicken farm located in the valley below. By instinct the chickens knew they must protect and care for the egg, so an old hen volunteered to nurture the large egg. One day the egg hatched and a beautiful eagle was born. But the eagle was raised to be a chicken. Soon the eagle believed he was nothing more than a chicken. The eagle loved his home and family, but his spirit cried out for more. While playing a game on the farm with some of his chicken friends one day, the eagle looked to the skies above and noticed a group of mighty eagles soaring in the skies. "Oh," the eagle cried, "I wish I could soar like those birds." The chickens roared with laughter, "You cannot soar with those birds. You are a chicken and chickens do not soar." The eagle continued staring at his real family up above, dreaming that he could be with them. Each time the eagle would let his dreams be known, he was told it couldn't be done. The eagle, after time, stopped dreaming and continued to live his life like a chicken never realizing that if only he would truly understand who he was and would spread his wings then he could fly like the rest of the eagles. Finally, after a long life as a chicken, the eagle died – a chicken. Don't limit yourself by thinking like a chicken when in reality you are an eagle. Be the leader you are by developing the skill of critical leadership thinking because as long as your mind is stuck with the followers you will always be the tail and not the head!

Everything begins with a thought. Therefore if I change my thinking, I change my destiny. Benjamin Disraeli said "Nurture great thoughts, for you will never go higher than your thoughts." Let's consider together the long term value of developing the art of a leadership mentality:

Great Thinking Challenges the Status Quo

Great thinkers are not content with things as they are because they always envision something better – something more. Mediocrity is not even in their vocabulary because to be mediocre means you are in the middle of the crowd. Leaders don't live in the middle – they live out in front! Great thinkers don't see things as they are – they see things as they could be. But they also know that the only way to get out of the state of mediocrity is to develop the habit of great thinking. William Arthur Ward said: "Nothing limits achievement like small thinking; Nothing expands possibilities like unleashed thinking." Too many times we feel trapped into leading like everyone else thinks that we must lead. We follow the paradigms that have been set before us as if we have no choice on whether or not to break those paradigms. I have found that the leader who has become a great thinker is not afraid to ask the question "Why?" Why do we do it that way? Why is that procedure in place? Why haven't we tried to accomplish this in another way? Through my experience of leadership I have found that people arbitrarily follow what is already in place simply because they have not taken the time to think through the process and possibly see a better and more effective way to accomplish the same result. God has called us to be effective in what we set our hands to do – which means we cannot accept the status quo but must be willing to challenge how we do things and even why we do them at all!

There is a well-known story of a mother and daughter who were working together in the kitchen preparing the Easter dinner. They always worked together to make their special traditional family Easter meal. No matter what the mother was doing, it seemed that the daughter was always watching her intently. The mother could even feel her daughter's big brown eyes on her without even turning to see if she was in the room. Yet she continued with her task of preparing the meal without even missing a beat or a blink. As she did every year the mother took the pan out of the cupboard and set it on the counter. Then she went to the fridge and removed the ham that had been defrosting. They had a large ham this year. It was not unusually large or different than last year's ham. She took the wrapping off and then proceeded to cut about an inch off of either end of the ham. Before the mother even put the ham in the pan the daughter stopped her and said: "Mom why did you cut the ends off the ham?" The mother stopped in her tracks and pondered the question. She was rather perplexed since no one had ever asked her why she cut the ham that way before. She had done it that way as long as she could remember. The mother answered her daughter and said: "Well sweetie, I really don't know the answer to your question. Your Grandma always cut the ends off of her ham and I have just naturally done the same thing. I never wondered why I did that though. So let's call Grandma and ask her why she cuts the ham that way." So they grabbed the phone and called Grandma. Then the mother asked her mother if she knew why she cut the ends of the ham off before placing it in the pan. The Grandmother stopped and became rather quiet. She hadn't thought about her ritual of cutting the ham being anything different than normal. Then it occurred to her that her own mother had done the very same thing for as long as she remembered. The Grandmother suggested that the daughter call her mother and ask her that very question. So she hung up the phone and dialed the little girl's great-grandmother. After the usual pleasantries she asked her why she cut the ends of the ham off before cooking it. She replied without hesitation and with a smile in her voice along with a little chuckle...... The reason that she cut the ends off of the ham was because back in the early days of their marriage she didn't have a pan big enough to hold the ham. They couldn't afford to buy a bigger pan either. So that was the only way to make the ham fit in the pan! What are you doing right now in your life that you have never questioned but rather simply do it because that is the way that it has always been done? Why haven't you taken the time to think it through and see if this is really the best way? Great thinkers challenge the status quo.

Great thinking draws great people into your life

You will never be surrounded with people who are greater than your level of thinking. We don't attract into our lives the type of people that we want – we attract the type of person we are! You cannot surround yourself by small minded people for they will extract the energy out of your ability to dream and envision a greater life. It is extremely important to find the people in your life whose ideas are creative and innovative and spend as much time as possible with them. The thoughts you have are not enough to take you to where you want to go. You must be willing to open your mind to the thoughts of others if you are to progress and grow. You will yield so much more innovation in your life if you are willing to collaborate with other good thinkers and add their thoughts and ideas to yours. There have been far too many times in my personal life of leadership where I withdrew myself when it was time to create something or be innovative in my leadership approach. For some reason I tended to think that in order to be effective and appear as the strong leader the ideas had to be mine and the vision must come from within. I have found that the most effective way to lead is to surround yourself with people who may see things from a different perspective than you and consequently add thoughts and ideas based on that different perspective. You must never lock yourself in to your own ideas because quite frankly – they are not enough. Johann Wolfgang von Goethe said: "To accept good advice is but to increase one's own ability." If you are not surrounded by people who are making you better then try making your thought life better. You will begin to attract people according to how you think; and through a collective thought process you will elevate your life and leadership to the next level.

Great thinking helps you learn more in life

Your education did not stop with your high school diploma or college degree. That was only the beginning of a life full of opportunities to learn and improve. But personal improvement comes by choice not by chance. Those who discipline their minds to think great thoughts will always be on the lookout for something new to learn – something that will bring improvement to life and add value to the life of others. Opportunities to increase knowledge abound for those who practice the art of great thinking. Their mind is always active and ready to receive new information which will inspire them to become greater than what they are. Great thinkers are great readers. They are students who carefully watch those who have mastered their craft in order to learn how they too can improve upon what they do. The greatest leaders are the greatest learners; but learning requires thinking. Change your mindset from being one who knows all the answers to one who will seek for more answers. Never become too much of an expert that you are unwilling to learn from someone else. Your mind is the compass that determines the direction of your life. Who you are today is the result of the thoughts you had yesterday. Who you will be tomorrow will be the result of what you think about today. Everything that happens in life begins with a thought. Every act of your life was first played out in your mind and as you pondered that thought it then became action. What we think determines what we do and what we do determines who we become. Who we become determines our legacy – therefore you can change the legacy of your life simply by changing your thinking! There are many things in life that you cannot change but your thinking is one thing that you <u>can</u> change and you <u>must</u> change if you wish to change your position in life. The Apostle Paul challenged us in Philippians 4:8: "Finally, brethren, whatsoever things are true, whatsoever things are honest, whatsoever things are just, whatsoever things are pure, whatsoever things are lovely, whatsoever things are of good report; if there be any virtue, and if there be any praise, think on these things." What you think about, you bring about. Therefore change your thoughts and you will change your life. Great thinking helps you learn more in life. Lest you think that changing your thinking is a difficult task I encourage you to consider the following:

Great thinking does not happen automatically

Too many people set their mind on cruise control and expect to end up in a beautiful place. Good thinking is the result of an intentional decision you make to control your mind and bring it into subjection to the thoughts that add value and growth to your life. When I was young I used to enjoy watching the old Laurel and Hardy movies. Every movie was a disaster waiting to happen. But the reality is that they simply didn't think about what they were doing which is why they always ended up in a catastrophe. Great leaders have mastered the art of intentional thinking. They don't allow their mind to wander into areas that are unproductive or unfulfilling. Great leaders don't allow their mind to be corrupted by the words of "experts" who think they know more about what God has called you to do – but in reality do not have the vision or the passion you have for who you are to be and what you are to accomplish. Be intentional about your thinking and reserve time each day to reflect upon where you are in life and what you have accomplished. Intentional thinking gives you a true perspective of your accomplishments and an honest evaluation of what you are doing well and how you can improve. You must be willing to evaluate each experience and put it in the proper perspective if you are going to grow and improve in all areas of your life. Experience alone does not teach you the lessons of life; only the experiences you are willing to evaluate teach you what you need to know. I like to reserve the early morning hours as a time of intentional thinking where my mind will reflect on all the current projects that lay in front of me and the needed steps to expedite and move those projects forward. Don't expect changed thinking to happen automatically. You must make time for intentional thinking. Reserve a place and a time in your day to focus your attention on what is most important. One of the most important pieces of counsel I have ever been given is simply this: wherever you are – be there. Don't be just physically there – be mentally and emotionally there. Don't disconnect yourself because you are unwilling to focus on that which is most important. Your life will end up a disaster simply because you choose not to think; therefore be intentional about what you allow in your mind!

Great thinking is the best investment you can make

Every thought is either a deposit or a withdrawal in your life. By thinking negative or condemning thoughts you are withdrawing energy and faith out of your life. By thinking positive and affirming thoughts based on the Word of God you are investing and depositing faith and energy into your life. The great news is that what you invest into your mind is played out every day through your actions. Therefore if your actions are to be positive and uplifting both to others as well as yourself then it must start with investing good thoughts into your mind. When you realize that thoughts become things and what you receive from life completely depends upon what thoughts you invest into your mind; it gives you an entirely different point of view about the methodology of your thinking. Each new idea that you allow into your mind is an investment into your future. Each new concept or dream can be a return bringing manifold blessing into your life. You have the power to create the world in which you live by the inspiration that God has given to your mind. I am a firm believer that being made in the image of God gives you that creative ability to build your future through the proactive thoughts given to you by the Holy Spirit. God already knows what lies in your tomorrow for He has already been there; therefore it is vital that you invest into your future by training your mind to think like God thinks and consistently look for ways that will improve your future and what He is doing in your life. You have one chance to complete your divine assignment. The worst thing that could ever happen to you is to come to the end of your life empty handed because you refused to invest in the most vital part of your being which is your mind. The choice really is yours: you can invest in yourself by choosing good thoughts or you can devalue your life by plaguing your mind with negativity. I choose to invest!

Great thinking will inspire those around you

When <u>you</u> change then the world <u>around</u> you changes. I am a firm believer that it is fruitless and pointless for you to focus on the things that you cannot change. Far too many people complain about things over which they have little or no control rather than harnessing and focusing their energy and creativity on things over which they do have control. You cannot control the weather outside your window but you can control the weather inside your mind. You cannot control the economy of the nation but you can control the economy of your mind. When people see that you have taken control of your thinking, you become an inspiration to them because of the changed life that you now exemplify to everyone around you. No one likes to be around someone who is gloomy, miserable and inconsistent. People will avoid you when they know you are tempestuous and unpredictable. But when you change your thinking – you change your countenance and your countenance is what adds value to the people around you. Positive and intentional thinkers add value and inspire others to become better and reach their full potential. How do they add value? It is very simple:

- **Great thinkers motivate great thinking in others.** When people see that you have changed then they now have hope that they too can change as well. Possibility and dreams lie in the visible example of a changed life!

- **Great thinkers inspire new ideas.** When those around you see that you add value to their ideas by giving a positive perspective then they will want to spend time around you. Every person loves to be with others who make their ideas look brilliant; be that person that others want to be with.

- **Great thinkers expand the world.** Every person wants to see more – do more – and become more. When you change your thinking not only do you expand your world but you also expand the world of those around you.

I reflect on Christopher Columbus and consider the dramatic impact he made on our world because he was willing to think beyond the conventional and limited thinking of his day. As he set sail into uncharted territory he did not have the answers of all he would encounter on his journey, but he knew that there was more of the world than what people had allowed themselves to think and he would prove it through this successful quest. Most people are inseparably tied to the status quo; they have never allowed themselves to see beyond the world they live in. That is why you must expand not only your world but the world of those around you as well. What an opportunity to create an expedition that will change our world. Let the journey begin now!

Look around you – are you bringing hope or despair to the people with whom you speak? Are they better as a result of being in relationship with you? Are you living in the same mental world that you lived in 20 years ago? What – if anything has changed in your approach to thinking? It is time to change your perspective and approach to thinking. You have the choice of what you bring into the confines of your mind – and please remember that what you allow in will eventually come out for "…as he thinketh in his heart, so is he" (Proverbs 23:7). Change your thinking and watch others around you change as well! Be a great thinker and you will be a great leader.

Chapter Five

Watch Your Language

Extraordinary leaders have extraordinary language. Leaders don't talk like followers; that's what makes them a leader. A leader lives at a different level of communication than do followers. That is so important for us to realize because the words we use provide a framework for meaning. People understand the world in which we live by the words that we speak. For someone to be able to clearly see where we are going – they must first clearly hear what we are saying. The words you say create movement in the environment in which you live. Your environment is created by the words that you speak because of the creative power that words possess. Hebrews 11:3 tells us that "By faith we understand that the worlds were framed by the word of God, so that the things which are seen were not made of things which are visible." God spoke and the invisible became visible. The impossible became possible. That which had never existed suddenly came into existence. How? Everything came to be by the power of His Word. When you look deeply into the Word of God you will find that all He has done throughout the history of the world is speak; everything He does is accomplished through the power of His word. Therefore you must not minimize the power of the words that you speak for right now they are creating the world in which you live. Think of the power of that statement. What you say today makes the decision of where you will live tomorrow. Every morning I make a prophetic declaration of what kind of day I am going to have. There are some days in which I declare that it will be a day full of wisdom and insight; all through that day I expect new insight to be granted to me because I have declared it to be so. There are other days in which I declare creativity to flow through my writing and lesson preparation. Other days are days of which I declare to be a day of connection. It is on these days when I have many meetings. I speak that there will be deep connections made through these meetings that will add value to my life and leadership. I believe in the power of my communication; therefore I have made communication – both written as well as verbal – a major priority in my life. With every word you say you are giving people an education about yourself. Your life is a living lecture series and what people learn <u>about</u> you determines how well they will learn <u>from</u> you. I will not learn from someone I don't trust or respect. Therefore it is extremely important that we decide to send the right message about who we are to those we are trying to lead; which means the words we use must be carefully <u>chosen</u> and <u>communicated</u> in order for us to gain trust and respect from the people we desire to influence. Without those two elements you lose both the right as well as the ability to lead. Choose your words carefully for you must live by what you speak. No doubt this is what the wise man had in mind as he wrote through the Holy Spirit in Proverbs 18:21, "Death and life are in the power of the tongue, And those who love it will eat its fruit."

Those Who Lead Well Learn to Speak Well

Great speaking is an ability that can be both taught as well as learned. Of the many great things you must learn – learning to speak well ought to be at the top of your list because quality people will not follow someone who does not have quality communication. John W. Gardner said, "If I had to name a single all-purpose instrument of leadership, it would be communication." The success of your leadership depends on your ability to clearly and consistently communicate to those with whom you work and over whom you have influence. According to experts, we are bombarded with 35,000 messages every single day! In an age of Facebook, twitter, text messages, RSS Feeds and communication from every source imaginable – it is extremely important that the great leader have the ability to <u>immediately</u> capture the attention of his listeners with meaningful messages that matter. Let's be honest – all the people we would look at as great leaders both from a ministry standpoint or a secular setting have all been great communicators. Who can forget the words of the following people who made history:

- **John F. Kennedy saying "And so my fellow Americans, ask not what your country can do for you - ask what you can do for your country."**

- **Winston Churchill inspiring a nation with "You ask, what is our aim? I can answer in one word: victory; victory at all costs, victory in spite of all terror, victory, however long and hard the road may be; for without victory, there is no survival."**

- **Ronald Reagan speaking in front of the Brandenburg Gate at the Berlin Wall saying for the entire world to hear: "Mr. Gorbachev, open this gate. Mr. Gorbachev, tear down this wall."**

We could continue forever with examples of leaders whose words inspired a revolution or a revival. It is amazing what misguided communication will do – even if the motive is right.

A couple from Minneapolis decided to go to Florida for a long weekend to thaw out during one particularly icy cold winter. They both had jobs, and had difficulty coordinating their travel schedules. It was decided the husband would fly to Florida on a Thursday, and his wife would follow him the next day. Upon arriving as planned, the husband checked into the hotel. There he decided to open his laptop and send his wife an e-mail back in Minneapolis. However, he accidentally left off one letter in her address and sent the e-mail without noticing his error. In the mean time: In Houston, a widow had just returned from her husband's funeral. He was a minister of many years who had been "called home to glory" following a heart attack (died and gone to report in heaven). The widow checked her e-mail, expecting messages from family and friends. Upon reading the first message, she fainted and fell to the floor. The widow's son rushed into the room, found his mother on the floor and saw the computer screen which read:

To: My loving Wife
From: Your Departed Husband
Subject: I've arrived!

I've just arrived and have been checked in. I see that everything has been prepared for your arrival tomorrow. Looking forward to seeing you then. Hope your journey is as uneventful as mine was.

P.S. Sure is hot down here!

Obviously the right communication said at the wrong time and to the wrong person will create disastrous results! To elevate your life you must have the ability to say the right things to the right people at the right time to create movement and action. If you expect people to move in the right direction, your communication must be:

- **Pointed** – I must get straight to the point and say exactly what I mean; not dancing around the issues but hitting it square on. Don't allow someone else to interpret what you say because most of the time their interpretation will be the exact opposite of what you intend. Be straight to the point.

- **Precise** – I must not use a lot of fancy language only to impress people. What good does it do if they are impressed by what I say but not inspired to do anything about it? The goal of communication is not to impress but inspire to action.

- **Passionate** – I must never merely communicate; I must connect. There is a big difference. Not all communicators connect with those to whom they speak; but all good communicators do! According to the *Harvard Business Review*, "The number one criteria for advancement and promotion for professionals is an ability to communicate effectively."

Effective communication will lead you to effective connection. When you make that emotional connection with people they will be much more inclined to hear what you have to say. Mental stimulation with no emotional connection will cause people to miss the premise and point of what you are saying. Not everyone may have agreed or heeded his message, but no one can deny that John the Baptist got the attention of people because of his passion. The next time you speak to people, observe their reaction. Are you connecting with them? Does what you say resonate with your audience? If you are not connecting – then are you really communicating? A catalytic leader will stand out from the crowd because of his passionate communication.

My question to you is: what do your words do? Have people become so accustomed to your communication that they have lost interest in what you have to say? If so – you have lost your ability to influence and without influence, you have no leadership. I encourage you to work on your communication skills this week. Read more – listen and watch excellent communicators – take to the pulpit or classroom this week with renewed confidence in who you are and what you have to say. People are looking for a reason to act – let what you say give them one!

What You See Determines What You Say

The reason that leaders speak differently is because they see things differently. We have already discussed the perspective of a leader, but let's take it one step further here by letting you know that how you see a situation will determine what you say about a situation. For example: if you call a problem a "big mess" or a "disaster" you will create within yourself a different set of emotions which will determine how you approach that problem. Instead of talking about problems as if they are hopeless and wildly out of control – the leader will use language like "opportunity" instead of "problem". He will call dilemmas a "challenge that will in some way make me a better person." He will use language promoting the idea of a solution rather than a stumbling block. Your words are powerful creators of emotion and how we feel determines what we do most of the time when we face challenges and difficulties. Be very careful about your choice of words when you are facing a difficult situation because your words will either build a bridge to a solution or they will build a barricade blocking people from seeing the solution. Your words will either <u>inspire faith</u> or <u>instill fear</u> into the lives of those who hear what you say. Learn the language of a leader and know that your mouth is subject to your mind; therefore what you see determines what you say. The same is also true with those you lead. What you say determines what they see. The perfect example of this is the 12 spies who Moses chose to spy out the land that had already been spoken for and promised to the Children of Israel. Now think about this for just a moment. This is land that God has already spoken a declaration of inheritance to His people. Yet as these spies are sent into a land that is technically and spiritually already theirs – they see two different things. Ten of these spies see giants while the other two see grapes. Ten of them see problems while the other two see possibilities and promise. Ten of them see a land that is beautiful, but yet out of reach. Two of them see a land that is already within their grasp. What they saw determined what they said as they came and gave their final report to the rest of the people of Israel. Your report to people decides your rapport with people. Listen to the Scripture: Numbers 13:27 states: "Then they told him, and said: 'We went to the land where you sent us. It truly flows with milk and honey, and this is its fruit. Nevertheless the people who dwell in the land are strong; the cities are fortified and very large; moreover we saw the descendants of Anak there.'"

These men saw both the grapes as well as the giants but chose to believe that the blessing of Canaan was not worth the battle to fight for that blessing. The problem I see here is that the people believed these negative and small minded spies due to the level of influence they possessed as chosen leaders from Moses. It was because of their negative influence that an entire generation of Israelites died in the wilderness without ever experiencing the best that God had prepared for them. Imagine that for a moment: an entire generation of people wandering in circles just miles from a land where they would enjoy the best of everything. All they needed was one more march across the border and they would be home in this beautiful country. But because of the negative impact of these words from the spies – they never made it. You must be careful about the force your words are going to bring to the people you are trying to lead. You are accountable not only for yourself fulfilling your potential and becoming all that God designed for you to be – but you are also accountable to motivate and equip the people around you to reach their potential and become all that they are designed to be. When you speak words laced with doubt or fear you prohibit people rather than motivate them, and you will be held accountable for that! Now listen to the words of Caleb in this same situation. Numbers 13:30 says, "Then Caleb quieted the people before Moses, and said, 'Let us go up at once and take possession, for we are well able to overcome it.'" This is the language of leadership! Caleb and Joshua <u>saw</u> the exact same scenario as the other ten spies – yet their focus was entirely different than the other ten spies. Sight and focus are two different things. Two people can see the same thing but have an entirely different focus. Rather than focus on the <u>difficulty</u> – Joshua and Caleb focused on the <u>reward</u>. The level of your focus determines the level of your faith. If you focus on the difficulties of life – your level of faith will be low because you will only see the mountain and not the faith that removes the mountain. But if you focus on the reward that lies beyond the difficulty – your faith will be great because you are motivated to receive and enjoy the reward. Leaders speak differently than followers.

- Leaders don't talk about stumbling blocks – they talk about "opportunities" or "challenges" that will bring improvement into my life."

- Leaders don't talk about problems – they talk about solutions.

- Leaders don't stop at asking questions – they look for answers.

- Leaders don't talk about failure because it doesn't exist in their vocabulary. Failure is merely a lesson on what not to do or how to do it better the next time you approach the same situation.

- Leaders calculate their words carefully because they know that once those words leave their mouth – they can never get them back.

What you see determines what you say – look carefully what is in front of you because it will eventually get inside of you. What is inside of you will eventually come out of the gate of your mouth which will have dramatic impact on the effectiveness of your leadership. I can listen to you for 24 hours and determine what kind of future you will have all because your <u>words</u> are creating your <u>world</u>.

Leaders Know that Language Can Be Learned

Of course it would do all of us well to be multilingual but I know that it will not happen with many people who are reading this book. So when I say that language can be learned – I refer to your ability to speak well can always be improved upon because solid leaders know that it is their ability to communicate that sets them apart from mediocrity. In fact I will go so far as to say that those who refuse to improve their ability to communicate seriously limit how far they will grow and consequently fail to inspire others to grow. It has been recorded that one of ancient Greece's greatest and most persuasive orators was Demosthenes whose first public speech was so feebly delivered and tortuous that his audience laughed him out of the Greek assembly. As he walked home disheartened and resigned to his inability to speak, an actor named Satyrus caught up with him and gave him a lesson in how to deliver a speech. Demosthenes then made himself an underground study where he stayed for weeks at a time practicing his oratory away from the distractions of the world. He cured a stammer by speaking with pebbles in his mouth and his shortness of breath by shouting out poetry while running uphill. With these efforts, he eventually acquired the ability to hold an Athenian audience spellbound and consequently become one of the most prominent of Greek statesmen and orators. It is imperative that you learn to speak well and speak with impeccability and integrity. Choose carefully not only what you say but the manner in which you say it. Always be aware of the impact your words are making through your tone of voice and the clarity of your words. If you don't predetermine the impact your words will have – you may end up having the wrong impact. Words are powerful. They can destroy a relationship – ruin a career or start a war. Don't ever minimize the power of your communication as a leader for your language will determine your level of success. Learning to communicate well is not difficult at all.

- **Read books written by great communicators.** Those who have the ability to communicate well also know how to write well. The more you read – the better you will speak. Reading sparks creativity and unlocks worlds you would have never known existed without cracking the book.

- **Make your thesaurus your best friend.** Don't be content with just the normal word, but find a word that more deeply expresses what you would like to communicate to people. Great communicators are always looking to expand their vocabulary.

- **Be certain that your communication connects with the heart of people.** The best communicators are connectors. They are people who move people to action because the words they use touch the heart of people – not just their head.

- **Watch great communicators.** Download their podcasts not only for the intrinsic value of their content but also for the value of their method of communication. I am careful to watch the facial expressions, body language, voice inflections and other methods that great communicators use. You will develop your own style but great communicators do have some basic styles in common and it will do you well to learn from those who communicate well.

Leaders speak a different language and it is a language that can be learned and developed. It is so true that people will judge you by the words you speak; therefore how well you communicate will often determine how well you lead. Good leaders know that talking is not enough but rather they do everything they can to make certain their words matter and make a difference. I don't want to communicate just for the sake of it. I want to know that what I communicate is adding eternal value to those who are the recipients of my communication. This is so important to me and I encourage you to make quality communication a high priority as well. I don't speak just to say something; I speak because I have something to say. Great communication brings great elevation!

Chapter Six

What You See
Is What You Get

The world's first operational atomic bomb was delivered by the Indianapolis, (CA-35) to the island of Tinian on July 26, 1945. The Indianapolis then reported to CINCPAC (Commander-In-Chief, Pacific) Headquarters at Guam for further orders. She was directed to join the battleship USS Idaho (BB-42) at Leyte Gulf in the Philippines to prepare for the invasion of Japan. The Indianapolis, unescorted, departed Guam on a course of 262 degrees making about 17 knots. At 14 minutes past midnight, on July 30, 1945, midway between Guam and Leyte Gulf, she was hit by two torpedoes out of six fired by the I-58, a Japanese submarine. The first blew away the bow, the second struck near mid-ship on the starboard side adjacent to a fuel tank and a powder magazine. The resulting explosion split the ship to the keel, knocking out all electric power.

Within minutes she went down rapidly by the bow, rolling to starboard. Of the 1,196 aboard, about 900 made it into the water in the twelve minutes before she sank. Few life rafts were released. Most survivors wore the standard kapok life jacket. Shark attacks began with sunrise of the first day and continued until the men were physically removed from the water, almost five days later. Within that number was a group of nine crewmembers who were pulled away from the fest of the ranks by the ocean current. Seeing these young men were beginning to lose their will, a young officer started asking them about their families and lives back home. He asked them to describe what they were going to do with their lives after they were rescued. He asked them about their spouses and children. He asked how they envisioned their parents must feel right now not knowing if they were even alive. With that discussion he encouraged them to fight to stay alive – not just for themselves but for their family's sake. He was inspiring them to envision life after this disaster; and it was the vision that kept them alive. Of the entire crew – two-thirds of the men perished in this tragedy; but all nine of these young men stayed alive and were rescued. Why? The answer is simple: they had a vision of what could become of their lives rather than where they were at the moment.

Every person must have a vision. The Bible is clear in Proverbs 29:18: "Where there is no vision, the people perish." Many people live idle lives without dreams or direction wondering why they are so unhappy and discontent. They watch other people succeed at the very things of which they know they are capable and wonder why they cannot succeed like others do. Night after night they sit in front of their television set squandering precious hours away with mindless entertainment muttering to themselves: "I work just as hard as the next guy! Why can't I have the money and the life that he does!" The answer is simple: they have never taken the time to envision themselves living the life God destined and designed for them to live. There is such power and passion in vision. There is nothing that is more important for those who want to succeed in life than carefully crafting and articulating a clear and compelling vision of who they would like to be and the level of life they would like to live. Without it you will aimlessly drift through life without direction and purpose squandering every opportunity that comes into your path. The most frustrating thing that I see in not only my own experience but in the experience of the people with whom I work and lead is the inability for us to clearly articulate the direction we are to go in life. Lack of direction gives birth to discouragement, and discouragement leads you into a seemingly endless cycle of failure and frustration.

You remember the questions you were asked when you were young: "What do you want to be when you grow up?" Without hesitation we would answer the question enthusiastically and describe with great detail exactly what we wanted to do as we grew older. The reason we could do that is because children have the ability to imagine things better than we do as adults. Somewhere between the innocence of childhood and the reality of getting married, raising a family, working to make ends meet, along with the other challenges that adult life brings to us we lose the ability to imagine the possibilities God can bring into our life. We lose that childlike capacity to believe that we can do the things that no one else says that we can do. The clouds of "real life" tend to block out the rays of sunshine that clearly show us the path that our life is to follow. For just a moment can you walk back with me to those days when we had the ability to imagine with the mind of a child? Can you go back with me into a childlike position where absolutely nothing is impossible? Jesus was very clear about the example of faith that a child brings forth when He said: "Verily I say unto you, Whosoever shall not receive the kingdom of God as a little child, he shall not enter therein." (Mark 10:15) So what does it take for you to create a vision that will compel you to greatness?

Vision Requires Imagination

Vision requires you to see something that is invisible. Helen Keller was asked once, "What would be worse than being born blind?" To which she responded, "Having sight without vision." This is where many people have a difficult time believing in the power of vision which quite honestly is what sets leaders apart from followers. Followers have a difficult time envisioning things that do not yet exist – but that is exactly what God did in the creation of this great planet on which we live. Genesis 1:2 reminds us that "…the earth was without form, and void; and darkness was upon the face of the deep." Yet in the midst of that darkness and chaos God "… calleth those things which be not as though they were." (Romans 4:17) Vision gives you the ability to see things as if they are already in existence before they are even started. I liken it to the example of a man who is building the home of his dreams. He already knows exactly where the kitchen is going to be; where his office is going to be; what kind of cabinetry is going to be in the master bedroom; the layout of his family room is already sketched in his mind; and he knows exactly where each fireplace in the home is going to be located. That man can take his friends to the ground on which his dream home is going to be built and he will easily give them a "virtual tour" of his home even though there is absolutely nothing that is there. He can point to exactly where his car will be parked in the garage – even though his friends may only see empty land and space. His imagination has already created the reality that is yet to come! As a leader you must be able to completely see what your organization or ministry is going to look like before it ever physically takes shape. You need to be able to envision the following:

- The type of people who will be on your team

- The type of people you will be reaching out to and serving

- The primary purpose and objective of why you exist

- The means and methods by which you will reach that primary purpose and objective

- The style of facility that will best make possible the fulfillment of your goals and objectives

When I accepted the pastorate at my present position I took upon the task of writing out exactly what type of church I wanted to pastor. I articulated on paper how I wanted our hospitality team to act when people came in the door; what I wanted the children's ministry department to physically look like; the values by which I wanted our leaders to conduct themselves and so forth. I tried to be as detailed and descriptive as I possibly could even down to how I wanted our hospitality team to dress. I knew that if I could see it in my mind before I ever acted upon it – then I would have the confidence needed to pursue my vision. You will never pursue anything that you first don't clearly see! I like the story of Hubert H. Humphrey when on a trip to Washington, D.C. in 1935, he wrote a letter to his wife in which he said: "Honey, I can see how someday, if you and I just apply ourselves and make up our minds to work for bigger and better things, we can some-day live here in Washington and probably be in gov-ernment, politics, or service...Oh, gosh, I hope my dream comes true – I'm going to try anyhow." If you can first see it – and then believe in the power of God to achieve it – there is absolutely nothing that can stop you. Allow yourself to imagine again!

Vision Requires Ownership

I firmly believe that vision cannot be taught; it must be something that comes from within. I know the question has always been asked: Does the leader make the vision or the vision make the leader? Great question and I believe the answer is simple: the vision must come first. The reason I believe that to be true is because there are many people who are filling <u>positions</u> of leadership but they have no vision. When a leader tries to con-tinue to lead without clearly articulating the vi-sion of where he desires to take the people, there is suddenly a lack of energy in the team; personal-ity conflicts become major battles and people be-gin to lose hope in the future of the organization. Vision is the most crucial element to any leader and to any organization; but the vision must start within the leader, requiring him to take a sense of ownership and responsibility. You cannot try to borrow someone else's vision because what worked for them may not work for you.

Vision is not something that is borrowed –
it is something that is birthed!

When you give birth to a vision this is the result:

- You can clearly articulate that vision with passion – there is no uncertainty because you see it so clearly.

- There is confidence within the people you lead because you are so clear about where you are going. When people feel secure that you know where you are going they will follow you with confidence and full support.

- Outward conditions including financial limitations do not sway you from pursuing your vision. The strength you have does not come from the <u>outward conditions</u> but rather from <u>inward convictions</u>.

- You don't allow what other people say to <u>affect you personally</u> because you are thoroughly convinced that this vision has come from within and just because someone doesn't understand it doesn't mean that it is not worth following.

True ownership of a vision comes only through times of deep introspection and prayer where you hear the voice of God directing you in a clear path. God uses the experiences you have already had to articulate a new vision and direction for you. He uses the present resources you have to determine the vision of where you are and where you need to go. He will also use the set of skills and gifts He has given you to create a clear vision of where you need to move in your life. God will never call you to accomplish something that He does not first equip you to accomplish. You cannot wait for someone to download or email you a vision for your life and leadership; you must search deep within your spirit to hear what God is saying. No one else knows the exact vision for your life. If you listen to the voices of others there will always be this sense of uncertainty and hesitation because the vision did not come from within. People do not follow leaders who are uncertain and hesitant! The Bible speaks clearly in 1 Corinthians 14:8: "For if the trumpet give an uncertain sound, who shall prepare himself to the battle?" You want your people to be ready to fight for your vision – but they cannot fight for something that you don't feel confident in fighting for. Confidence only comes through ownership – so do you own your vision or is it simply being borrowed from someone else?

Vision Requires Unwavering Commitment

Once you find it – take ownership of it and protect it with all of your heart for there will be many who will come and try to distract or distort the vision for your life. Circumstances will arise that will attempt to lead you away from who you are to be and get you involved in activities that are not bolstering and strengthening your vision. You cannot allow that to happen. One of the greatest examples of unwavering commitment to a God-inspired vision is the Old Testament character of Nehemiah. Although he was not even in the city of Jerusalem to see the broken down walls and desolation with his physical eyes – Nehemiah still was able to see the vision of what needed to happen with his spiritual eyes. The city had lay in ruin for 120 years after the Chaldeans had torn down the walls. (2 Chronicles 36:19) Literally thousands of people had physically seen the need to repair the walls but no one did anything about the need simply because they lacked the vision needed to undertake such a seemingly insurmountable task. The city was not only vulnerable to her enemies because of the disrepair but also it gave reason for the neighboring cities and countries to scorn and mock the city and its inhabitants. There is no beauty in a vision which lay unfulfilled. It is no wonder that as Nehemiah heard the terrible news of his homeland and the disrepute that had been placed on his own people as a result of the desolation that he wept and fasted and prayed a prayer of sincere repentance to the God of His people. (Nehemiah 1:4) A perfect example of taking ownership of a vision is found in the prayer of Nehemiah when he said: "Let thine ear now be attentive, and thine eyes open, that thou mayest hear the prayer of thy servant, which I pray before thee now, day and night, for the children of Israel thy servants, and confess the sins of the children of Israel, which we have sinned against thee: both I and my father's house have sinned." (Nehemiah 1:6) He wasn't even there and he was not part of the problem; but he definitely wanted to be part of the solution which is how the vision was born. Once he arrived on site – there was no going back. He was stanchly and steadfastly committed to the task at hand. Even when Sanballat, Tobiah, and Geshem the Arabian, who were the enemies of not only the vision but also the people of God, tried to set up a meeting with Nehemiah causing him to cease from the work he was doing – his response was very clear: "I am doing a great work, so that I cannot come down: why should the work cease, whilst I leave it, and come down to you?" (Nehemiah 6:3) They tried four different times for him to stop what he was doing so they could meet together but each time Nehemiah gave them the exact same response. His commitment to the vision of rebuilding the walls of Jerusalem was stronger than the convenience of taking a break – even for just a short while. When you have genuine ownership of a vision there is absolutely nothing that can take you away from the fulfillment of that vision. The strength of the desire within you outweighs any pull that outside sources or circumstances may try to bring against you. This results in an unwavering commitment that will accomplish what seemingly is impossible in such a short amount of time with what may seem like a short amount of resources. Nehemiah was able to complete this work in only 52 days because he was able to rally his people around a vision of a great tomorrow. When they saw that he was willing to actually leave the Palace in Persia and identify with the problem by traveling to Jerusalem – they bought in to his vision and fulfilled it with a commitment that was unyielding. Vision requires unwavering commitment.

What desires and passions are burning within you today? As you look back at your life what have the experiences of your past taught you and developed within you? Can you honestly answer what tools and abilities God has equipped you with? Can you clearly see where you are going and how you are going to get there? All of these questions are imperative for you to answer if you are going to elevate your life with the power of vision. This is a most crucial element to living at the next level, for without vision – your dreams, desires, and plans will die and be wasted in an imagination that never became reality. Don't let it die today but rather reignite the vision that is within you. See the dream and then seize the reality!

Chapter Seven

You Will Never Go Up Until You Grow Up

You will never reach a level of excellence and effectiveness higher than your willingness to grow and change. A leader who is unwilling to grow will suddenly find himself without people to lead. People are looking for leaders who can take them to places and levels they have never been because in reality – most people are not content with where they are in life but they simply do not know how to get out from where they are to another level; consequently they look for leadership to lead them and guide them to a greater dimension in life. The problem comes when leaders are unwilling to change and grow which in turn stifles the growth and development of the people they are attempting to lead. Your greatest challenge in life is to keep yourself on a plan of perpetual growth and development so that you can in turn inspire others to do the same.

Ecclesiastes 10:10 tells us: "If the ax is dull, and one does not sharpen the edge, then he must use more strength; but wisdom brings success." The 16th President of the United States, Abraham Lincoln said, "If I had eight hours to chop down a tree, I'd spend six hours sharpening my ax." If you do not keep yourself sharp – you will be unable to effectively lead others into a position enabling them to succeed. The problem that many people have is that they think growth and development is automatic; unfortunately – that is not the case. Growth and development are the results of a conscious decision to do the things necessary to insure daily change in your life and in your leadership. Unless you first change what is within you – you will never change what is around you. The tendency of most leaders is to see all of the things that need to change within their organization or ministry.

- They see the shortfalls of the personnel involved in the organization and attempt to immediately make the needed changes in staffing.

- They see structural or governmental changes that need to happen and they instantly go to work on the structure and makeup of the organization.

- They see flaws in the vision or mission of the organization so they go to work to form a creative committee to generate a new mission statement for the group.

- They see budgetary concerns that have limited the ability of the organization to grow so they construct a brand new approach to the group's financial overview.

On and on the list could go of the immediate changes that become visible to the proactive leader; and without question, all of them are both needed and important. But the most important change that must come first is the change within the leader. You cannot <u>effect</u> change until you first <u>experience</u> change. The ultimate test of your ability to lead will come through your ability to change yourself before you try to change others. That ability comes only through your decision to put yourself on a plan of perpetual growth and development. As Dr. John Maxwell has said so many times: "Change the leader, change the organization." Your ministry or organization will never grow or change beyond your willingness to grow or change. You are the thermostat that sets the temperature for the people you lead. If your people are cold and indifferent – take a hard look at yourself and see if there is a chill or spot of indifference within your spirit. If your people are stuck in a rut – get out of the leadership car you are driving and see if you have been spinning your wheels as well. If your people are resistant to new ideas – then stop for a moment and consider what new thoughts or ideas you have recently resisted. It is time to **be** the change you desire to see in others.

You cannot expect more of others than you expect of yourself because people are led by <u>example</u> – not by <u>explanation</u>.

Therefore – the questions you must ask yourself are these: What is my plan of personal growth? How am I developing as a leader right now? What ideas or concepts have I resisted in the past that I need to embrace if I plan to move forward? Am I doing the same things over and over again but somehow expecting different results? Consider carefully these thoughts with me as we desire to experience positive change in our lives so that we can effect positive change in the lives of those we lead.

Growth is Not About What You Do

When we think about growth and change we typically think about the first things we must <u>do</u> in order to bring about that growth. Growth is not a doing process – it is a becoming process. We are not called "human doings" – we are called "human beings".

The first question you must ask when considering how you can grow and be successful is simply this: What must I <u>become</u> in order to achieve that level of leadership for which I am striving? What you do in life is only an outflow of who you are. If you become the right person – you will never have a problem of achieving the right things. I believe in the power of setting goals as the primary source of accomplishment for those who achieve great things in life. But so many people set goals that end up somewhere in a graveyard of unfulfilled dreams and objectives and they are continually discouraged at their lack of ability to achieve what they set out to do. They then try to set higher goals and perpetuate loftier dreams; only to once again be disappointed at their lack of ability to keep their commitments. I have come to the conclusion that it is not the goals that must change – it is the person who must change; it is your discipline and dedication to follow a carefully laid out plan. In order for your life to change – you must change. If you don't like what you are getting from life – than you need to change who you are. Les Brown has written, "To achieve something you have never achieved before you must become someone you have never been." Real success is not a doing process – it is a becoming process. It is a metamorphosis that is best described by the Apostle Paul when he wrote in Romans 12:1 "And do not be conformed to this world, but be transformed by the renewing of your mind, that you may prove what is that good and acceptable and perfect will of God." Growing is a transformational principle of changing our process of thought so that we can become a person of action; for until the mind changes – nothing else in your life changes. No one can change what is in your <u>hand</u> until they change what is in your <u>head</u>! You will never harvest better and richer fruit in your life until you are willing to nurture greater thoughts in your life because thoughts are the seeds that grow into things.

It is important for you to realize that you will attract what you want in life by the person you become. You will attract the people you want in life by the person you become. When you improve – your situation improves. When you get better – the things around you get better. Jim Rohn wrote this great statement: "The most important question to ask on your job is not "What am I getting?" The most important question to ask is "What am I becoming?" Growth is not a doing process – it is a becoming process!

Growth is a Learning Process

I have found that those who grow the most have many things in common but there is one that stands above the rest: they each have an insatiable appetite for learning. They are constantly reading new material; attending more seminars; listening to more teaching and lessons; talking to, and more importantly, listening to others who have achieved success. This journey of becoming better is a journey of <u>education</u> more than <u>inspiration</u>. It is very easy to get inspired; all you need is a motivational speaker who is able to rouse emotions up within you getting you fired up to go change the world. The problem with motivation is that it is not enough. If I don't know how to act on that motivation I feel – I will be more <u>excited</u> than I was yesterday – but not more <u>educated</u>. It is education that sets people who succeed apart from those who willingly stay the same way they have always been. When I say education – of course I am not only speaking of formal education received in the classrooms of universities and institutions of higher learning. Degrees and diplomas are good and quite necessary – but it is <u>self</u> education that makes the most difference in the life of a "difference maker." It is the man or woman who is willing to invest the needed time to learn something new every day that will rise to the top faster than the person who is merely content to stay at the same level he or she has always been. It is amazing how some people will seemingly work hard yet never reach that level of fulfillment and success of which they know they are capable. They may remind themselves of how hard they work and how dedicated they are to their job, but the difference lies in that the successful person will be the one who comes home and works on <u>himself</u> after he has worked on his job. Those who grow are those who read; those who listen and learn; those who are constantly looking for new concepts to sharpen their leadership skills. They are the ones who take the course on better communication. They are the ones who go back to school to gain the degree that will propel them further in their career. Growing is a process of learning. If you are not learning something new –

then you are not growing. When you stop learning – you stop leading. The best leaders are the best learners. My challenge to you is simple: **Put a process in place that will put you on a path of continuous learning.** Learning is a process that is accomplished on a daily basis.

"What you're doing daily is determining what you're becoming permanently." - Dr. Paul Crites

Permanent success will be found in your daily agenda. There is no person that becomes an over-night success or sensation; it just doesn't happen. For those who seemingly achieve instantaneous success – it is always short lived because they never went through the process of developing a daily routine that insured continuous learning and improvement. That is why lottery winners who may win millions of dollars will many times end up going broke. They lost the need to improve themselves; therefore they squandered the wealth they received and ended up worse off than they were before they won the lottery. Set habits and routines of personal growth into your daily agenda. The first hour of the day is the best time for you to spiritually and mentally get challenged and inspired because you are fresh and the slate of the day is completely clean. Your first hour of the day is the rudder that determines the course and direction of the rest of the day. Use the time to inspire and motivate yourself to learn something new. Make a prophetic declaration of what the day is going to bring to you. Your habits determine your future; therefore set daily habits in place that will lead you to grow and your future will be bright. Growing is a process of continual learning.

When U.S. Supreme Court associate justice, Oliver Wendell Holmes Jr., was hospitalized at the age of 92, President Roosevelt went to visit him. He found Holmes reading a Greek Primer. "Why are you reading that?" the president asked. The great jurist replied, "Why, Mr. President, to improve my mind." Here are decisions you can make right now that will set you on a path of perpetual growth and learning:

- Choose and make provisions to be part of a seminar this year led by successful people in your field of leadership from whom you can glean insight and instruction.

- Schedule time in your daily activities in which you will listen to a lesson that directly applies to an area in which you need to grow.

- Set a goal of learning something new every day and then share what you have learned with someone else. It is by sharing new insight that causes it to solidify within us.

- Choose people to mentor you. A mentor is simply someone who has been where you have not been. Therefore a mentor can be someone you personally know or even a leader you follow through books, teaching, seminars, etc. A mentor is someone who is willing to transfer the information and experience he or she has gleaned in order to expedite your journey to where they are right now. I like what Dr. Paul Crites wrote about a mentor in his book <u>21 Things Every Leader Needs to Know</u>. He said that there are three things your mentor represents: an exit from your present – an attitude of confidence toward your future – and accountability in your life. Your friends are comfortable with your present but a mentor is comfortable with your future. A mentor in your life can prevent you from making costly mistakes that may hinder your progress to where you want to go in life.

- Firmly believe that it is your duty as a leader to constantly improve yourself. If your development and growth is a part of your belief system then it will be a priority in your daily routine because we only act on those things that we truly believe. Your belief will determine your behavior. What you believe about yourself will determine how you live. If you truly believe that growth and development is the only way to survive in the jungle of leadership then it will be a high priority in your daily routine. You have probably heard the definition of insanity: doing the same thing over and over and expecting different results. If you don't change your <u>routine</u> then you will never change your <u>results</u>!

The questions are simple: How will you live your life? Will you live the way you are living right now? Will you continue to surround yourself with shortsighted people who never see beyond their present position? Will you continue to listen to people who speak only of life as it is and never life as it could be? Will you stay in the same position of mediocrity you are in right now? You can choose at any moment and in any situation to grow and become better. Development is a choice – it is a well thought out decision that many times will come from people who finally say to themselves: Enough is enough! I am tired of living far short of my potential. I know that there is more within me that I have not yet been able to pull out. Anyone who has ever succeeded has reached this point. They have come to the point of their lives where they draw the line in the sand separating themselves from what they have been and what they can be. Some people will draw this line when they are young – many not until they are older. Most people will draw it more than once. The point is that each of us must come to the point where we are no longer content to live as we are because there is a voice that is crying deep within us to be something more. We want more than <u>success</u> – we long for <u>significance</u>. It is a human endowment given by God for our lives to matter and mean something. We are not created to merely survive but rather created to thrive. But to reach that point you must be willing to do whatever is needed to grow and get away from the position of mediocrity in which you now find yourself. You must be willing to learn new skills – change what is not working – develop your gifts beyond their normal ability so you can join those for who normal is not enough. You are tired of being average – tired of blending in with the rest of the world and playing it safe – tired of being just another name on the roster. This is the position in which those who commit to developing themselves beyond normal finally reach, and this eventually sets them apart. Now is that time for you. I pray you are ready to put yourself on that plan that will take your life out of the realm of the ordinary and into the realm of the extraordinary. Growing leaders become great leaders!

Chapter Eight

Coloring
Outside the Lines

Creativity means operating your life at <u>maximum</u> speed and performance. Creative people open the throttle and live at full speed. They are not tentative or hesitant in their leadership. They don't approach vision and leadership with timidity but rather when they know the direction they are to move they do so with veracious vigor and vitality. Of course the faster your speed in your life leadership – the more mistakes you will make. That is okay. You know that the faster you travel down the highway – the higher probability of having an accident. Now I am in no way advocating speeding on the interstate the next time you travel; but when it comes to leadership we must be much bolder in the direction we move. We must be willing to make mistakes and fall down sometimes. All great leaders and innovators have been people who have made many mistakes but what separates the successful from the mundane and average is that they have the ability to see past their mistakes and visualize a more creative approach to accomplishing the task and reaching their goals. If you are afraid of making mistakes then you are afraid of being successful. I will deal with this topic of failure later in this chapter. The point is that the faster you travel in life the more prone you are to making mistakes; but creative people cannot stand to do anything halfhearted or at half speed. With creative leaders – it is all or nothing. Either you are in or you are out. Of course that is the way Jesus wants you to live your entire life. He rebuked the Laodicean church in Revelation 3:15-16: "I know thy works, that thou art neither cold nor hot: I would thou wert cold or hot. So then because thou art lukewarm, and neither cold nor hot, I will spue thee out of my mouth." Most people reading this enjoy a beverage that is either hot or cold. But one that is tepid is flat and stale; definitely not enjoyable and relaxing. That's why the waitress keeps adding hot coffee or fresh iced tea to our cups and glasses – to keep things fresh. Creativity keeps your leadership fresh by adding new thoughts, ideas and concepts. Creativity motivates you to try new theories that may not be popular or in the "norm" so to speak. Creativity sparks ideas that have not been tried by anyone else because no one else can lead your people like you do. You know where they are in life; you know what it takes to reach them and motivate them to reach their full potential. You know their struggles and setbacks and as their leader you know what it takes to move them in a forward direction. That is what leadership is all about. But that requires <u>you</u> live and lead at full speed. The progress of your ministry or organization depends on the speed at which you are willing to come up with creative and innovative ideas that will maximize both your personal as well as your corporate potential. You cannot continue to lead at the pace you have always led and expect your organization to grow! But it is important to know that if you are going to live and lead with the throttle wide open – you will need to create a culture that generates as little friction as possible. Friction is the resistance that one surface or object encounters when moving over another. If you plan to move forward you must do everything you can to remove or at least reduce friction from your life and from the organization you are trying to lead. Sometimes friction comes from <u>problems</u> and sometimes it comes from <u>people</u>. You have to be able to identify the source of friction and quickly move to resolve that friction so it does not hinder the speed at which you desire to move. At what speed are you living and leading right now? Push the pedal a little harder and see what happens. Creative people live full speed ahead.

Creativity means loving what you do and doing what you love. When you stop loving what you do it is time to move on to another project because you will never excel at that which you don't love doing. To <u>excel</u> at what you do – you have to <u>love</u> what you do. That is a novel idea that we all know yet so few people follow that ideology. Many have the idea that the days of carefree playing and having fun ended when they graduated from high school and moved into the "real world." What in the world does that mean? Didn't you live in the "real world" when you were a child? Of course you did. It was as real as the world you are living in right now – the only difference is as a child your primary objective was to seek after activities that brought joy and ful-fillment to your life. You didn't worry about paying the mortgage or somehow making certain there was enough money left at the end of the month. You loved life and that was all that mattered! I was re-cently playing outside in the grass with my young-est son, Connor, when I realized something. The fact that unemployment in the United States is at an unbelievable rate of 9.6% didn't bother him even in the least bit. As I threw him in the air and watched him giggle with delight – I realized that his fun was not deterred at all by the fact that the national debt is almost at a staggering 13.5 trillion dollars. As we rolled trucks down the driveway together, Connor acted like he didn't have a care in the world – be-cause he really doesn't. When I tucked him in his crib for a restful night of sleep I realized that Con-nor fully expects to wake up to a hot breakfast, clean clothes, more than enough toys to play with, and most of all, a family who loves him more than life itself. I thought to myself: when did that love of life change? Is it because we become more "mature" in our approach to life? As I contemplate all of this I think I understand a little more of what Jesus meant when He said, "Assuredly, I say to you, whoever does not receive the kingdom of God as a little child will by no means enter it." (Mark 10:15). Of course Christ wasn't asking you to go back to your childish ways of spilling your soup and forgetting to make your bed. He was asking you to return to the simple yet profound way of thinking that you did when you were a child. Keep in front of you things that inspire and motivate you. Use the right pictures and music that produce ingenuity and creativity within you. You should be doing what you love and loving what you do – because without intense pleasure in what you do you will never be able to have intense production from what you do. Those who are creative have this childlike love for who they are and what they are called to accomplish. Don't ever lose it!

Creativity means believing that you can do absolutely anything you set your mind to doing. God has given you the incredible ability through your thought life to create a vision of what can be and then work towards manifesting that vision within your life. Because you are created in the image of God you then have the nature and characteristics that God possesses. You see things that don't yet exist but you are living them in your dreams as if they do exist. That is what you do every single night when you dream. That is how a creative person lives his life <u>every</u> <u>single</u> <u>day</u>. You must firmly believe that if you have the ability to conceive something in your spirit then God will give you the creative ability to fulfill that which you set your mind to. Relentless faith and belief in the impossible is imperative if you choose to elevate your life to the next level. You must be willing to put all of the misconceptions about yourself behind and start to believe in the things which you have struggled to believe in the past. If you are not living a life motivated by dreams then you are stuck in a rut of normalcy. I hate normal. Every creative leader hates normal. Normal is not in his or her vocabulary because normal blends in with the rest of the world around you. I intentionally chose the title of this chapter to be <u>Coloring Outside the Lines</u> because that is what creative people do. I refer again to my three year old son, Connor, who is just learning to color at this stage of his life. I don't expect him to color perfectly inside the lines. He is unleashing the creative side of himself which means I celebrate whatever he creates and the more I celebrate with him the more creative he becomes. It is interesting to note that 90% of five-year olds see themselves as highly creative; that in itself is not amazing, but wrap your minds around the concept that by the age of seven, 80% of us who saw ourselves as creative no longer believe we are. That means only 10% of seven-year olds believe they are creative. By the time we reach our teens that number drops to 2% and remains fairly constant throughout our adult lives. Pablo Picasso believed, "Every child is born an artist. The problem is how to remain an artist once he grows up." Don't limit your creativity by limiting your thinking. Whatever you think is possible is in reality possible and that is the principle by which all creative leaders must guide their life each day. How do you do away with thinking that limits you? Here are 5 simple steps:

Change your system of belief

Ask yourself the question: What do I believe about myself and the world around me? Write it down on paper. You may not know that you are limiting what you can do and become because of a deep seated set of beliefs about yourself that have hindered you from moving forward in life. You may catch yourself thinking or saying such statements as: I am not good enough; I could never do that; I don't have enough money; I just haven't been given the right opportunity; I am too old to start over. If any of these thoughts become part of your thought pattern or vernacular then you have limited yourself by an improper belief system. You will never change what you accomplish in life until you are willing to change what you believe about life. Your belief system is the core of who you are; it is the definition of what type of person you have chosen to be. Your belief system is not just a set of ideas that you possess; it is a set of ideas that possesses you. These ideas define you and identify who you are as well as who you are not. Who you are will obviously translate into what you do because our level of behavior is determined by our level of belief. When you begin to see yourself as capable of much more through the power of God and His Word you will then begin to see a change in your ability to believe in others as well. Amazingly you will see their level of performance increase because they will live up to your level of belief in them. Your goal should always be to move from a victim mentality to a visionary mentality. Victims talk about the problems of their life while visionaries talk about the possibilities of their life. Visionaries create and inspire while victims gossip and complain. Now is the time to change your belief system by formulating a Biblical model of thinking about yourself and the world around you; just see if you release a newfound creativity within you.

Change your environment

Creativity can be stifled by the wrong environment. A creative environment can be like a greenhouse where plants are delicately nourished and cared for until the seed becomes a fully grown beautiful plant. The right environment will release a creative energy within you that will flow from the concept of idea to implementation. I love to be able to call the creative team of leaders from my church together and for us to brainstorm new ideas on reaching our goals and living out our values. As the ideas begin to flow a synergy begins to develop between the team members and ideas flourish. The more the ideas flourish the stronger the team members become in their personal lives as well as in our lives as a team. As creativity grows your team members grow; as your team members grow your entire organization grows. Don't ever stifle the creativity of your team by not providing a healthy and creative environment in which they can thrive. Remove the negative drains in your work environment. Some may not just be physical drains but emotional drains as well. Don't allow gossip and criticism in your work place. Create a system of values by which your team will be defined. It is that system of values that will establish the environment in which you work and create. Every team member needs to have the ability to clearly define that set of values and live accordingly. When everyone is on the same page concerning what will define your team then an environment will be created that fosters teamwork and creativity. Environment is such an important element to develop as a leader because people are looking for the right setting in which they can thrive; it is up to you as the leader to create it – not stifle it.

Embrace Off Beat People

Creative people can be a little eccentric at times. Their habits and routines may not be ordinary; but I have found that ordinary people are not creative people. In fact ordinary and creative can rarely be used in the same sentence! (Although I just did that!) Off beat people have the ability to take a good idea and make it better. They really don't care about the status quo which is why they are willing to challenge the establishment. If you are going to elevate your life to the next level you must be able to appreciate people that others think are odd. It is so important to surround yourself with highly energized and creative people because they see things differently than the norm. Elevating to the next level means exactly what it says: it means you don't stay at the level that everyone else is living and leading – but rather you move above where they are so that you can lead them somewhere they have never been. But that requires you to surround yourself with people who don't think like everyone else thinks; because if they did – they would be standing on the same level as everyone else. Don't be afraid of bringing people around you who don't think like you do. I have people on my leadership team that see things differently than I do and I love that type of tension. Tension is good because it forces you to release your predetermined ideas of how things work and move totally into a realm you have never before explored. That tension will come when you embrace creative people who bring things to your attention that you would not otherwise see. Learn to embrace these people and there is no limit to what level you will be able to lead. When you have a variety of people who surround you at the table ideas flow – inspiration streams into reality – and innovation takes off into a new dimension.

Challenge Your Level of Innovation

Creative leaders are innovative leaders. We all know by now that leadership is not tied to a position or title. For those who think that their title qualifies them to be a leader – there is a rude awakening in their future when they find out that people have no desire to follow someone who is wrapped up in himself. If you desire to continue to be a leader people desire to follow – you must practice innovative leadership. You may ask "Aren't all leaders innovative?" One would think that is what elevated them into that position of leadership in the first place. But there are certain things you must do to remain innovative in your leadership and ministry. Here are a few thoughts:

- **Stay Flexible** – An innovative leader and pastor is never content to accept or live with the status quo. There will be things that you try – programs that you implement – that simply don't work. An innovative leader does not throw up his hands in disgust and walk away but rather is flexible in his thinking and approach to leadership, knowing that when something doesn't work it only means that there is a better method out there to reach the desired result. What are you currently doing in your ministry or leadership that is not producing the desired results? Schedule a meeting with your staff or team of leaders and ask the question of why it is not producing. Then look at creative alternatives to changing the approach to the program or eliminating it all together.

• **Stay Energized** – Innovation takes energy. When you are consistently looking for new ideas and methodology it requires an intense amount of creative energy – not just mentally but even physically. Doing something physical every day boosts your brain function, fuels higher energy levels, and helps you manage stress more effectively. Get the amount of sleep that you need each night and shut your mind down when you go home from the church or office. Look for natural ways to increase your energy level. I have never seen an innovative leader that does not maintain and exude a significant amount of energy. Energy is contagious and will increase not only your effectiveness but the effectiveness of those around you. Start a routine of physical exercise and activity this week. Put it in your To-Do list or goal tracking system and be faithful. Go to bed earlier so that you can get up earlier. Make the decision today to replace some of the junk food that you regularly eat with a diet that will increase your level of energy and focus.

- **Stay Positive** – Innovative leaders aren't perfect but they just learn more from their mistakes. The only way for you to maintain the right level of innovation and creativity is to maintain a positive outlook on life and leadership. Optimism is crucial because it builds the momentum you and your team need when things don't go as planned. Beyond momentum, optimism keeps your perspective open to new ideas, which is the basis of successful innovation. People want to follow a leader who believes in what God has called him to do and believes in the people he is leading! Take five minutes right now to assess your attitude. Do you walk into your church or your office with a smile on your face? Do you look people in the eye and greet them by name? What tone of voice do you use with people on your staff or team? Make a conscious effort to be optimistic in all situations. Optimism is not a feeling – it is a choice!

There is no greater time than right now to become a creative leader. Stop looking at life as black and white and add some color into your vision. You are an amazingly creative person because God made you that way. Start leading as you were created to lead and you will find that leading is an adventure that is outlandishly exciting and electrifying. Normal is out of style...learn to hate normal!

Chapter Nine

Who's Around You
Eventually Gets in You

Who you know determines what you know and what you know determines where you go. There is a greater power to produce that comes when you are able to find the right people with whom to partner your efforts because you were created by God for partnership. When God looked at Adam – His crowning creation – the first thing He said about him was: "It is not good that the man should be alone; I will make him an help meet for him" (Genesis 2:18). God created a partner not from outside of Adam but rather from his innermost being by taking a rib from his side because we partner best with those who have the ability to work alongside of us with the same mindset – the same goals – the same purpose that we have. Eve came from the inner confines of Adam which made it easy for them to partner together. "And Adam said, This is now bone of my bones, and flesh of my flesh: she shall be called Woman, because she was taken out of Man." (Genesis 2:23) This was literally a marriage made in heaven! The first thing that God told them after this divine partnership was put into place was "Be fruitful, and multiply, and replenish the earth, and subdue it:" (Genesis 1:28). Man was created to be productive. When I don't produce – I miss the purpose of my existence; and when I don't have purpose – I don't have the passion to live. Many people are living meaningless and hollow lives because they have failed to produce anything of significance. They have become consumers but not producers. God never intended for you to live your life strictly as a consumer but created you both with the propensity as well as the ability to produce. He also set forth the principle from the very beginning that the only way we can effectively produce is through divine partnership with those with whom God brings to us in the course of our lives. If you fail to surround yourself with the right people then your ability to produce what God wants to produce out of your life will be ineffective and futile at best. You cannot produce without the right partnership. Even the very Son of God knew the value of selecting the right people to be part of His ministry team. Before He ever started His public ministry here on this earth the Lord spent a night in prayer seeking the will of His Heavenly Father because if you choose the wrong people to be on your leadership team –

not only will it <u>hinder</u> your effectiveness – it will <u>handicap</u> your effectiveness. The Lord set the perfect example through spending a night in prayer because too many times our human perspective gets in the way of our spiritual discernment. We look at the outward characteristics of people and judge them according to fleshly criteria. We think that because they look like a leader or even act like a leader that we must choose them to be part of our leadership team. Even the most Godly and spiritual individuals can make this mistake and get caught up in the earthly approach to looking at people. Samuel was looking for the new leader of Israel when God called Him to go to Jesse's house in Bethlehem because God had chosen one of the sons of Jesse to replace the backslidden Saul as King of Israel. (1 Samuel 16) Samuel was in the right <u>place</u> and even with the right <u>people</u> – but he came with the wrong <u>perspective</u>. As Jesse's boys were lined up for Samuel to examine, the Bible says in 1 Samuel 16:6, "And it came to pass, when they were come, that he looked on Eliab, and said, Surely the LORD's anointed is before him." Based only on outward appearance and attractiveness – Samuel had made up his mind who God had chosen to be king. "But the LORD said unto Samuel, Look not on his countenance, or on the height of his stature; because I have refused him: for the LORD seeth not as man seeth; for man looketh on the outward appearance, but the LORD looketh on the heart." (1 Samuel 16:7) We cannot use *earthly* criteria to make a *spiritual* choice. Samuel was a great man of God on whom the Spirit of God rested; but the moment he used human wisdom in making a choice of leadership – he missed it. Just because a man or woman looks like a great leader or even talks like a great leader does not mean that God has chosen them to be the ones with whom you partner. The people with whom you surround yourself will either increase or decrease your level of life and leadership. I have found people will either elevate your effectiveness or eliminate your effectiveness. Your circle of partners will determine how far you go and who you become when you get there. Ray Kroc, the brains behind the success of the McDonald's franchise, said: "You are only as good as the people you hire." That is a powerful statement to consider! The people around you will determine the level of your success. Robert Malone, a good friend of mine, has always told me: "Show me your friends and I will show you your future." You will find that having the right people with whom to partner is one of the most valuable lessons in leadership and life you will ever learn. Without partnership – you will never produce. Here are some lessons I have learned about partnership that I want to pass along to you:

You Must Value the Right Partnership

He who thinks he can accomplish anything of significance by himself has deceived himself. There is no such thing as "The Lone Ranger" when it comes to succeeding in life and leadership. Significance is found not in what **I** can do but rather in what **we** can do together. As has been said by many – all of us is better than one of us. The wise man Solomon wrote: "Two are better than one; because they have a good reward for their labour. For if they fall, the one will lift up his fellow: but woe to him that is alone when he falleth; for he hath not another to help him up. Again, if two lie together, then they have heat: but how can one be warm alone? And if one prevail against him, two shall withstand him; and a threefold cord is not quickly broken." (Ecclesiastes 4:9-12) Only a fool thinks that he can effectively navigate through this complex journey of life and leadership by himself. You will always place a high priority on the things you value. You can know the value a person places on their physical health by the foods that he eats as well as the amount of time he exercises in a week. You know how much a person values his job by both the number of hours as well as the disciplined effort he shows on the job. The value of a person's marriage is defined by how much they communicate and spend time with their spouse. You give respect to that which you value. Therefore – if you value the people with whom you are surrounded – you will respect them and place a high priority on insuring that you always have the right people around you. Insecure and controlling people don't value partnership. They have this sense that by bringing other people around them it will in some way limit their ability to control; and by losing control, they lose their authority. This is so typical of a person whose only influence lies at the positional level. If you were to take away their position or title – they would lose all of their ability to influence. As has been said many times by the great Dr. John Maxwell: "Leadership is influence. Nothing more; nothing less." Positional leaders tend to be more insecure; always worried about someone becoming better than they are or taking something from them. One of the greatest decisions you must make as a leader is to place a high value on having the highest quality of partners to work with you. A Chinese proverb states: "Behind an able man there are always other able men." Look at where you are right now. If you are not advancing and moving forward in life and leadership – it may be because you have not placed a high enough priority on bringing the right people into your life. When you learn to value what other people bring to the table you will find that what they bring completes what you already have. You must begin to perceive people as those who <u>complete</u> you rather than <u>compete</u> against you; by so doing your assessment of people will drastically increase. The only way to <u>discover</u> the right partnership is to <u>value</u> the right partnership. Do you enjoy working with other people? If not, why not? What do you lack in leadership that can be brought into your life by finding the right people? Have you taken the time to seek out the right people? The proof of what you value is found in what you pursue.

You Must Appreciate the Right Partnership

People thrive in an environment of appreciation. They suffocate in a controlling and unthankful environment. Too many times leaders who are production driven will fail to realize the greatest production comes from working with the people with whom they are surrounded. You must never forget that they are not working <u>for</u> you – they are working <u>with</u> you. When you have the mindset that they work for you then you fail to appreciate the gifts and the talents they bring to the table because you begin to view your people only as a tool to be used to propel you at a quicker rate toward your desired destination of success. People are not <u>tools</u>, but rather they are God-given <u>gifts</u> to you who bring the needed elements into your leadership that will elevate you quicker and higher than you could ever do by yourself.

Think about this for a moment. What if someone were to give you the gift of a brand new black, sleek and sporty Mercedes? It is a vehicle you have been eyeing for a long time thinking to yourself, "Man, wouldn't I look sharp driving that car?" It is something about which you have been dreaming and praying that someday that dream would become a reality. Suddenly one day, seemingly out of nowhere, someone walks up to you and hands you a set of keys. Guess what – they are the keys to that sleek and sporty Mercedes you have been dreaming about for so long! Now – what is your reaction? You are elated and you might even hug the person who has been so gracious to give this gift to you. You sincerely appreciate what they have done because not only will you be driving down the highway – but you will be driving down the highway <u>in style</u>! You look better – you get to where you are going faster than you normally would – and you feel good about yourself all because of the gift of the Mercedes that person has given to you. Even as you read this right now – you can already feel the leather seats and all of your sensory stimuli are going crazy as you imagine yourself driving that dream car. You cherish that gift!

Now consider: that is exactly what the people who God has brought into your life and leadership do – they are a gift that makes you look better and gets you to where you need to go faster than you could ever get there by yourself. The right people and partners will help you reach the pinnacle of success in style! But like the gift of the Mercedes – you need to learn to <u>appreciate</u> the gifts that the people around you bring to the table. They offer different gifts than what you possess which is why God has brought them into your life. If they have the same gifts that you have then you wouldn't need them! Learn to appreciate the differences between the people on your team. Identify the gift and skill set they possess and compliment them regularly on the value that they bring to your team. Don't focus on the negatives of your leaders, but focus on the positive energy and ability that they add to your overall mission and objective. If they are not adding positive energy and ability then quite possibly you have the wrong people at the table. The point that you must accept is that appreciation of people will go much farther and keep people much longer than criticism and condemnation. In his book *I Ain't Much, Baby – But I'm All I Got*, Jess Lair comments: "Praise is like sunlight to the warm human spirit; we cannot flower and grow without it. And yet, while most of us are only too ready to apply to others, the cold wind of criticism, we are somehow reluctant to give our fellow the warm sunshine of praise." I sincerely believe if you will learn to show earnest and heartfelt appreciation for those with whom you serve you will unlock treasures within them that they did not know existed. Most people live only a fraction of their full potential. There is so much more to unlock in the hearts of people but that potential will not be unlocked through statements which find fault or minimize their strengths. People do not respond to a negative or critical spirit but they do respond to someone who recognizes their value and sincerely compliments their value. Learn to appreciate your people and you will find in turn that they will appreciate you.

You Must Discover the Right Partnership

There are specific people God has chosen to work with you in leadership. There are certain personality types that you must have surrounding you that will make you better than what you are right now. There are certain gifts that you don't have (and that is okay that you don't have all the gifts!) that others will bring to your table of leadership. Be convinced that there is a team out there who can be brought into your life for the purpose of fulfilling that which God has called you to do. But the right partner will not come by accident; they will come by intentionality. You must determine that you will do whatever it takes to <u>attract</u> and then <u>keep</u> the right people around you so you don't miss the opportunity God has placed in front of you. This is crucial because who is <u>around</u> you will affect what is <u>within</u> you! Discovering the right people you choose with whom to serve begins with <u>you</u>. You need to be very clear what you are pursuing in your life and leadership because you will need to surround yourself with people who are clear about where you are going and have the ability to add – not detract – from the direction you desire to go. But if you aren't clear where you are going – then how in the world can anyone else be clear?

Clarity creates security. When people are clear about who you are and where you are taking them – there is a sense of safety that they will experience and everyone knows that people perform best when they feel safe. Imagine having to work in a hostile environment where mortar shells are dropping all around you and you hear the sound of tanks rolling up outside of your office. I don't think that makes a favorable environment for a productive and creative staff meeting simply because you don't feel safe. Innovation thrives in an environment of security. The clearer the picture is painted to your people – the more secure they will feel and consequently the better they will perform.

Clarity unlocks creativity. When the mission and objective are clear, a sense of creativity is suddenly unlocked because people see the finished product or project in their mind before they ever put pen to paper. Each person has a strong innate and God-given ability to be creative; so the great leader will seek to unlock that ability within the people who surround him putting them in an environment that is clear and free from ambiguity. The clearer and more concise your vision, the more creative people will become in pursuing and capturing that vision.

Clarity promotes unity. When people are clear about why they do what they do there is a unity that brings a tight bond because everyone knows that their role – no matter how small or seemingly insignificant – is contributing to a larger picture that is worth celebrating. There is nothing that unites a team more than having a few wins under your belt and then celebrating those wins together. When people are clear about the direction you are moving then they will unite with you and fight for your cause because they believe in where you are going.

I have given you these values of clarity because in order for you to discover the right partners you must be very clear about who you are and where you are going. Clarity starts with you and trickles down to everyone around you. Are you clear about your values? Do you have a clear and compelling vision for your life and leadership? What are the values that characterize the ministry or organization that you lead? How do you live out those values in your everyday life? What are the objectives you hope to achieve through what you do? These are questions you must be able to clearly and distinctly answer if you are going to attract the right people into your life. Here is the cold hard reality: we don't attract who we want – we attract who we are. Therefore – if I am to attract the right people – I must become the right person. Right now take the time to think about these questions:

1. **What attributes would you expect out of the people with whom you work?**

2. **What character qualities are you looking for in finding the right people?**

3. **What level of work ethic do you desire in the people with whom you will surround yourself?**

4. **Describe the relationship you wish to have with those whom you surround yourself.**

5. **What leadership and life philosophy or vision do you expect the people around you to maintain?**

6. **What type of home life do you want them to have?**

All of these are essential questions you must ask as you pursue finding the right people for your team. But after you answer those questions – it is now time to look at yourself and ask these hard hitting (and even harder to answer) questions about yourself:

1. **Do you possess and live out the attributes that you would expect from those who surround you?**

2. **What kind of leader would attract the level of people that you have just described through the above questions?**

I go back to the earlier statement that I have made: you don't attract who you want in life – you attract who you are. You will not attract people who are more passionate about the cause of your organization than you. As the leader you are the thermostat that sets the level of temperature for your organization and you will draw people who are either at your level of passion or <u>below</u> it. Therefore – to attract great leaders you must become a great leader! It is important that you detail all the qualities and attributes that you need to work on in order to facilitate and lead other great leaders. Rather than <u>pursue</u> the right people – passionately <u>become</u> the right person. Pursuit is elusive. Therefore stop pursuing people and begin developing yourself and the right people will come to you.

Create an Environment of Partnership

Your environment will either <u>stimulate</u> or <u>stagnate</u>. Your environment will either <u>motivate</u> or <u>manipulate</u>. People do not like to be manipulated. People long for the freedom to become all that they were designed and created to be and it is up to you as a leader to create that environment where the creative nature of the people with whom God has blessed you is developed and not diminished. When you have the ability to unlock the potential of the people who surround you then the potential that lies within you will skyrocket to new heights because when you unlock their potential it only increases your ability to succeed. An environment of partnership is so important simply because:

- **Partnership increases productivity.** When you surround yourself with creative people the energy and resources needed to accomplish your goals and vision is magnified. Woodrow Wilson said, "I not only use all the brains that I have but all I can borrow." You will never have an environment of productivity without an environment of partnership. Nurture the abilities that people bring to the table because they will magnify what is already there and increase your ability to produce.

- **Partnership increases perception.** The people with whom you are surrounded will see things differently than you do – which is a good thing. Never lock yourself into the thinking that your perspective is always right. I have learned the hard lesson in ministry and leadership that I need to make decisions based on a diversity of <u>perspectives</u> because I am leading a diversity of <u>personalities</u>. If everyone in the world perceived life and leadership as you do then it would be a very dull and boring world! I love the story of the six blind men who were asked to determine what an elephant looked like by feeling different parts of the elephant's body. The blind man who feels a leg says the elephant is like a pillar; the one who feels the tail says the elephant is like a rope; the one who feels the trunk says the elephant is like a tree branch; the one who feels the ear says the elephant is like a hand fan; the one who feels the belly says the elephant is like a wall; and the one who feels the tusk says the elephant is like a solid pipe. Each one is convinced that they have accurately described what an elephant looks like but only based on their perception of that elephant. Finally the king explains to them: "All of you are right. The reason every one of you is telling it differently is because each one of you touched a different part of the elephant. So, actually the elephant has all the features you mentioned." Learn to embrace diverse perception and you will be able to make wiser decisions.

- **An environment of partnership increases potential.** The greatest leader is one who is more concerned about each person's potential in life than he is about their position in life. Positions are short lived and highly overrated. A position can be taken away at a moment's notice and the person is left wondering what just hit them. But potential is something that will last with people forever.

Potential is a gift – one that is to be cherished, nurtured and developed. A good leader will create an environment where people are encouraged to grow and develop. They are motivated by an ongoing personal growth and development program within your organization. This type of environment stimulates people to become better because they genuinely feel as though the leader believes in their ability to perform and grow. At the core of every human being is a longing for someone to believe in them. You will never realize the impact of creating an environment where growth and potential is a priority. Michelangelo, when questioned about his masterpiece David, answered that the sculpture had always existed within the stone. He had simply chiseled away the rock around it. Every person has been brought to you for a reason. It is time that you as a leader step up and see the potential that lies within that person and do whatever necessary to "chisel" away what has covered the masterpiece of their potential. There must not only be opportunities for growth but the needed encouragement from you as the leader. Awaken the hunger for significance which exists in your people by creating an environment in which their potential is stimulated and not stifled.

Environment is everything. Plants will not grow unless they are planted in healthy soil and receive just the right amount of sunshine and precipitation. People will not grow unless they are planted in the right environment of appreciation, vision, and development. You set the temperature of the environment of your organization and your world. Your people will never be more passionate than you are about the vision of your organization. Therefore – determine today that you will change the environment in which your people lead. You will be amazed that by changing the environment you will change your partners. As the old saying goes: Birds of a feather flock together. Great leaders attract other great leaders. When great leaders and their creative minds come together in a visionary environment phenomenal things will happen. Look around you today and ask these questions:

- Who do you have surrounding you?

- Are the people with whom you partner making you better or are they bringing you baggage?

- Is it easier to lead with the people you have around you or has leading become more challenging because you have the wrong people at the table?

- Are the people around you adding value and motivating or are they demotivating and taking your organization in the wrong direction?

- Are the people around you making your load lighter or do you find them adding weight to your leadership responsibility?

Every person in your life is doing one of two things: either they are motivating you toward your destiny or they are manipulating you toward doubt. You cannot feed a dream and feed doubt at the same time. The people with whom you are surrounded will feed something. If you don't have the right people at the table feeding you the right things then it is time to make a change. Change your partners and you will change your productivity. Increase the level of your partners and you will increase the level of your potential. Now is the time to realize the power of partnership!

Chapter Ten

Called
to be a Catalyst

Every leader worth following is earmarked by an insatiable appetite to see the organization over which he or she has leadership and influence **consistently move in a <u>forward direction</u>.** Leaders cannot stand to take even one step backward. Going back never enters the vocabulary of the successful leader. There is nothing to go back to! I have always been amazed at the attitude of the children of Israel after God miraculously delivered them out of the bondage and slavery of Egypt. One would think that these people would be forever grateful not only to God but also to the leader chosen by God to deliver them from a life of horrible bondage to the good life of living in Canaan. It would seem obvious after seeing God take out the firstborn of every household in Egypt, except the Jewish households whose doorposts were covered by the blood of the

Passover lamb, that they would be forever appreciative for their miraculous deliverance. I would personally think that coming to the Red Sea and being trapped between a body of water that you cannot cross with a vicious enemy hot on your heels and breathing down your neck, and then suddenly seeing the hand of God amazingly divide the water allowing you to walk across on dry ground, would cause you to be forever indebted to Jehovah. God continually showed the Israelites that He was intent on moving them forward into a better place...yet I am astounded by the attitude they maintained after seeing such miracles. The Bible states that the Israelites complained to their leader by saying: "Because there were no graves in Egypt, hast thou taken us away to die in the wilderness? wherefore hast thou dealt thus with us, to carry us forth out of Egypt? Is not this the word that we did tell thee in Egypt, saying, Let us alone, that we may serve the Egyptians? For it had been better for us to serve the Egyptians, than that we should die in the wilderness."

This is an attitude every leader is required to face at some point in his or her leadership: people are more willing to live in the past – even if it means risking the loss of reward or progress – rather than moving forward to a greater future. That is why every leader must have the desire to be a catalyst for change. Real leaders **need** to see progress; it is an unexplainable spark within them that motivates them to do what they do every day. Simply defined by the Merriam Webster Dictionary – a catalyst is a **substance that enables a chemical reaction to proceed at a usually faster rate or under different conditions** (as at a lower temperature) than otherwise possible. My translation into our realm of understanding is that the leader is an agent that provokes or speeds significant change or action. Of all the obligations and responsibilities that you have as a leader – one of the greatest is that you must be a catalyst for change in your organization. You must take the responsibility to **make** things happen within the organization you lead. You cannot wait for the environment to be right or the season to change. You must take the initiative to see the directives that will produce the most out of the organization and inspire the needed changes to make that happen.

There are four steps I would like to share with you that each leader must take in order to cause the needed reaction to bring the right change.

1. Catalysts Initiate

2. Catalysts Inspire

3. Catalysts Think It Through

4. Catalysts Are the "Go To" People

Allow me to share what I mean about each of these:

Catalysts Initiate

Catalytic leaders do not wait for the perfect time and season to do something. When they see a need they are motivated to do whatever it takes to meet that need. Jesus was the greatest Catalyst of all time. When confronted with 5,000 men who had sat under His teaching all day long and were now hungry, He told His disciples, "**You** give them something to eat." He was teaching His disciples that they were responsible to make something happen to meet this need. **A catalyst doesn't just have good ideas – they have the discipline and desire to <u>move</u> on those ideas and make things happen.** Too many times we have meetings where creative and innovative ideas are brought to the table – but then we leave the table and fail to act on those ideas. Catalysts always think, "What is the next <u>actionable</u> thing I can do to bring this idea to pass?" If I do not act then I will be acted upon; and the result of someone or something else acting upon me is never the same as if I had taken the initial action to make something happen. Every person who is a catalyst brings a certain intensity with them that inspires people to action. We have had our fill of ideas; it is the implementation of those ideas that will bring the needed change to your organization. What project lays in front of you waiting on your action? Take the first step today to initiate this project towards its completion. Pick up the phone, schedule the meeting, write out the plan – just do one step today to make this happen! What goals have you set for your organization or personal life that have never been reached? Is it because the ideas needed to reach that goal never made it out of the conference room and on to someone's "To Do" list? Good intentions can never be the substitute for action. Thomas A. Edison said it well when he said "Vision without execution is hallucination." There are too many inspirational ideas that never saw the light of day because of our unwillingness to initiate the implementation of those ideas. Right now I challenge you to look at the projects that lay either on your desk or in your mind. What is the first thing that you can do to initiate the implementation of that project? Do you need to make a phone call, write an email, schedule a meeting, or make an appointment? The key is to do something today to get the ball rolling. Don't wait on the perfect time or the perfect season for that may never come. The people following you are waiting on your first move and the moment you make that move your team will follow you. You may be surprised at the results of just one small step of action. Catalysts initiate.

Catalysts Inspire

We live in a generation where leadership and ministry have become scarred because of scandal and improprieties. The world is tired of pastors and leaders failing morally, financially bilking people out of their investments, or simply taking advantage of the position they have been given. They are desperately looking for individuals to inspire them to greatness. A true catalyst is one who – at the moment they walk into the room – bring with them a sense of excitement and inspiration. Many times – they do not have to say a word; it is simply their presence that brings a level of expectation into the room. One of the greatest needs people have is for someone to inspire them to become greater than what they are at this moment. I know very few people who are completely satisfied with where they are in life. They are looking for someone to spark a flame within them that will motivate them to move from where they are to a greater level in life. **You are that spark!** But you cannot spark someone else unless there is a flame from within to ignite that spark! You cannot inspire someone else to become greater unless you are inspired yourself. You know as well as I do that leadership has very little to do with title and position; it has everything to do with influence. So here is the question: Are people inspired by you? Do your words and your passion bring an excitement to the people you are around or is it more of a "ho hum" feeling that you leave with people? To begin with – let me encourage you to think about the answer to these questions:

- Who has inspired you in your life?

- What did they do and why did it inspire you?

- Who might you inspire? (Don't limit yourself to those you lead. Think of those within your home, other leaders in your community or someone who sees you often)

- Are you providing the example you desire?

Your example is the greatest means of inspiration you can provide. It is not necessarily what you say – although as we have already discussed communication is important. But it is more important to focus on **being** the right person rather than merely **doing** the right things. People are inspired by the spirit and passion you carry about who you are rather than what you are doing. Think about it – aren't you inspired when you see someone loving who they are and what they do? I am inspired when I hear preaching that comes from the inner depth of the preacher's spirit. I am inspired when I see an athlete give that extra effort that makes his performance remarkable. I am inspired by even a waiter at a restaurant that loves what he/she does so much that extra service is something he actually enjoys giving to you. The list goes on and on. The bottom line is this: determine today that you will live each moment with the goal of inspiring and motivating those around you to become greater. Be remarkable at whatever you do and people will sit up and take notice. Most importantly – you will inspire them to be remarkable as well. What an incredible way to elevate your life!

Catalysts Think It Through

One of the primary and most needed characteristics of a catalyst is that they are able to see things that others don't see; they can sense something that quite possibly no one else will ever sense. As a result of that sense, they will move quicker and in a more decisive manner than anyone else, which will move those with whom they have influence into a better position to win. You must not wait for your team to see the need – you must be the first one to see it and then take responsibility to act on that which you see. That is why after the college football game on Saturday afternoon you will find the head coach being the one who goes to the office and begins to review game film for the following week's opponent. He is the one who must take responsibility to see what his players don't see so that he can develop the needed strategy that will lead his players to win. Coaches win games before the clock ever starts; it is won during the many hours of watching game film and formulating a strategy based on what they see. The game is won during the long hours spent on the practice field not only talking about strategy, but playing it out over and over again until it becomes like second nature to the players. Legendary college football coach Bear Bryant said: "It's not the will to win, but the will to prepare to win that makes the difference." In order for your leadership to be earmarked as catalytic you must have the will to think long and hard about the direction you are going and then move without fear in that direction. Many people feel like catalysts are people who act only according to intuition and are spontaneous in all that they do. But I have found that the greatest catalysts who have sparked a revolution or revival are those who have prepared and planned precociously and then acted upon that plan courageously. Jesus told us in Matthew 14:28-30 "For which of you, intending to build a tower, sitteth not down first, and counteth the cost, whether he have sufficient to finish it? Lest haply, after he hath laid the foundation, and is not able to finish it, all that behold it begin to mock him, Saying, This man began to build, and was not able to finish." The catalyst sees the finished product before he ever drives the first nail which is what makes him look as if he is acting with ease and without thought. When a team sees the leader moving seamlessly ahead there is an excitement created within them to move forward and support the leader who has given them the needed spark to succeed. The reality is that the catalytic leader has given much thought and thorough planning – that's why it almost seems as if he effortlessly moves in the direction of success for his team. What a great position to be in! It has been said that we must think like a person of action and then act like a person of thought. Catalysts have the ability to think it through and then act it out. Lead your team by action – not reaction!

Catalysts Are the "Go-To" People

Catalysts are the "above and beyond" type of people. They are the people out in front leading the charge toward victory. They are the ones to whom people look when questions or crisis comes. When the game is on the line the catalyst is the one who wants the ball because he knows he is the one who can make the winning shot or score the winning goal. The time for you to become a catalyst is now. Your team depends on it for without a catalytic leader you will be in for a losing season! Decide at this moment that you will do whatever it takes to become a catalyst. Put yourself on an intense personal growth program. Get out of your comfort zone. Do something you have been scared to do in the past. Do whatever it takes to change your mindset from merely being a "player" to becoming a catalyst. Take your life to the level of a catalyst by becoming someone who initiates and inspires. Carefully think things through then act courageously on what you have planned; determine to be the "go-to" person when the game is on the line. Now is the time for **you** to be the spark that lights up your organization. I guarantee that not only will you elevate your life – the lives of those around you will elevate as well.

Conclusion

My objective and desire in this book has been very simple – to inspire and motivate others to carefully examine the potential that has been placed within them by a loving God and do everything they can to maximize that potential whereby they can most effectively live and lead. Leadership starts with yourself. Much of what has been written in the previous pages has been directed so each of us can carefully examine the ability that we already possess and then add to that ability the tools needed to take full advantage of what God has brought into our lives. This is a great moment to lead. I realize that we are living in very dangerous and uncertain times. There is a moral and spiritual battle in which we are engaged in this last hour. The economy has created a level of stress and anxiety that is unprecedented from any other time in world history. People are living in fear because of the uncertainty of tomorrow. What greater opportunity than that for someone just like you to step up and lead with integrity, character, and vision! This is an exciting time to be alive and an even more exciting time to lead. People are crying out for strong and persuasive leadership; they long for someone to inspire hope and a greater perception of what God can bring into their lives. We cannot leave it to the secular world because the premise on which the world around us attempts to lead is faulty and futile at best. There is a need for Godly leaders to come out from their sequestered corner and stand with vigor and vitality and declare that there are still strong men and women who will stand on principle and back that principle with the practice of everyday living and leading. Don't minimize the moment; but rather realize that like Esther – you have been called for such a time as this. I stand with you as a rallying cry and strong voice encouraging and inspiring each of you to make up your mind that now is the time and this is the place that you have decided to elevate your life and leadership to the next level. Walk with me, my friend, for there are mountain peaks yet unclimbed; territories yet unclaimed; and battles yet to be fought. Thank you for being one who not only reads but readies himself to accept the challenge. I look forward to walking with you and celebrating with you as you elevate your life with renewed purpose, commitment and vision. This is the time to see your life elevated!

About the Author

Dr. Mark Lantz is a professional speaker and pastor whose driving mission in life is to inspire others to reach their full potential through passionate communication and personal influence. He is a firm believer and proponent of each person's ability to achieve to a higher level and position in life through personal growth and development. Dr. Lantz serves as Senior Pastor of Christian Center Church in South Bend, IN as well as director of World Harvest Ministers Network. He is an avid student of the heart of leadership and personal growth and loves to share inspiring principles to churches, leadership organizations, as well as both civic and corporate organizations. He just completed a curriculum of lessons based on this book designed to improve every person's ability to raise the level of their life or leadership skills. Mark received his Doctorate of Ministry in 2012 from Indiana Christian University and is on a journey to inspire as many as possible to the greatness God has placed within them. He is happily married to his best friend Crystal and is the proud father of Wesley, Austin, Kelsea, and Connor. If you want to learn more about Mark and see what's on his mind and what drives him every day, follow along and connect on Facebook and Twitter or visit his website: www.drmarklantz.com